T0341891

TRADITION,
SCRIPTURE, AND
INTERPRETATION

EVANGELICAL *RESSOURCEMENT*
ANCIENT SOURCES FOR THE CHURCH'S FUTURE

D. H. Williams, series editor

The Evangelical *Ressourcement:* Ancient
Sources for the Church's Future series is
designed to address the ways in which
Christians may draw upon the thought
and life of the early church to respond to
the challenges facing today's church.

TRADITION, SCRIPTURE, AND INTERPRETATION

A Sourcebook of the Ancient Church

EDITED BY

D. H. WILLIAMS

Baker Academic

a division of Baker Publishing Group
Grand Rapids, Michigan

© 2006 by D. H. Williams

Published by Baker Academic
a division of Baker Publishing Group
P.O. Box 6287, Grand Rapids, MI 49516-6287
www.bakeracademic.com

Printed and bound by CPI Group (U) Ltd, Croydon, CR0 4YY

All rights reserved. No part of this publication may be reproduced, stored in a retrieval system, or transmitted in any form or by any means—for example, electronic, photocopy, recording—without the prior written permission of the publisher. The only exception is brief quotations in printed reviews.

Library of Congress Cataloging-in-Publication Data
   Tradition, Scripture, and interpretation : a sourcebook of the ancient church / edited by D. H. Williams.
       p.   cm.
   Includes bibliographical references.
   ISBN 10: 0-8010-3164-8 (pbk.)
   ISBN 978-0-8010-3164-9 (pbk.)
   1. Christian literature, Early. 2. Theology—History—Early church, ca. 30–600—Sources. 3. Church history—Primitive and early church, ca. 30–600—Sources.
   I. Williams, Daniel H.
   BR160.A2T73 2006
   230'.13—dc22   2006016598

Unless otherwise indicated, Scripture quotations are from the Holy Bible, New International Version®. NIV®. Copyright © 1973, 1978, 1984 by Biblica, Inc.™ Used by permission of Zondervan. All rights reserved worldwide. www.zondervan.com

CONTENTS

SERIES
PREFACE

THE EVANGELICAL *RESSOURCEMENT*: Ancient Sources for the Church's Future series is designed to address the ways in which Christians may draw upon the thought and life of the early church to respond to the challenges facing today's church. The term *ressourcement* was coined by French Roman Catholic writers in the mid-twentieth century as descriptive of theological renewal that declared Christians must return to the sources (*ad fontes*) of the ancient Christian tradition. The operative assumption was that the church is apostolic (formed and directed by the Old and New Testaments) and also patristic (indebted to the intellectual and spiritual legacy of the fathers of the church). Much of our understanding of the Bible and theological orthodoxy, directly or indirectly, has come through the interpretive portals of the early church, which is an integral part of the Protestant identity, no less than it is for Roman Catholicism or Eastern Orthodoxy.

Using the methods and tools of patristic scholarship, each series volume is devoted to a particular theme related to biblical and theological interpretation. Similar to the past practices of *ressourcement*, this series is seeking to appropriate the contributions of the early church not in an idealized sense but through a critical utilization of the fathers as the church's primary witnesses and architects for faithfully explicating the Christian faith. Series readers will see how (1) Scripture and the early tradition were both necessary for the process of orthodox teaching, (2) there is a reciprocal relationship between theology and the life of the church, (3) the liberty of the Spirit in a believer's life must be balanced with the continuity of the church in history, and (4) the Protestant Reformation must be integrated within the larger and older picture of what it means to be catholic. In effect, it is the intention of this series to reveal how historical Protestantism was inspired and shaped by the patristic church.

As Protestantism confronts the postdenominational and, in many ways, post-Christian world of the twenty-first century, it is vital that its future identity not be constructed apart from the fullness of its historical foundations. Seminal to these foundations is the inheritance of the early church, "that true, genuine Christianity, directing us to the strongest evidence of the Christian doctrine" (John Wesley). Therein Christians will find not a loss of their distinctiveness as Protestants but, as the sixteenth-century Reformers found, the resources necessary for presenting a uniquely Christian vision of the world and its message of redemption.

PREFACE

WHEN FIRST ENCOUNTERING the life and thought of early Christianity (end of the first to the fifth century), students and correspondents often ask me where they should start. There are many fine books available on the early fathers, as well as a few that make the perilous attempt at explaining the fathers' significance for today's church. Some are better than others, but there is no doubt that a new hunger for the church's ancient legacy is swelling within Protestant ranks, calling for reliable guides to the world of the early church.

Of course, there is no substitute (and never will be) for reading the ancient sources themselves. Without knowing firsthand what the ancient fathers really taught, there can be no reliable application. With a good English translation, contemporary readers will be surprised at how much they can comprehend from the primary texts themselves, even if the reading also raises many questions. Just as it is far better to read Matthew or Paul than to look at what a recent commentary says about Matthew or Paul, it is better to read post-apostolic writers such as Ignatius of Antioch, Cyprian of Carthage, and Gregory of Nyssa than to read *about* them. Students of the Bible and seminarians are usually taught this principle of priority, but sometimes expediency (the writing of a paper or preparation of a sermon) gets the better of them. Even some scholars yield to this temptation.

For the novice, there are two "risks" in reading the ancient texts. (1) The amount of material to be read, especially works by fourth- and fifth-century writers, may seem overwhelming. Writers in antiquity were not nearly as concerned with expediency as modern readers are.

9

(2) A great deal of the material may seem strange and not immediately relevant to our understanding of Christianity. We may or may not find much to "apply to our lives." There is indeed great spiritual treasure and theological insight in the corpus of the early fathers, but these riches are not usually on the surface of the text. Deep speaks to deep. Even short or abbreviated passages require patient and thoughtful consideration (*meditatio*). Understanding the writings of the early church is like encountering another Christian world, accessible to the general reader yet calling for a willingness to be taught and led into foreign places of the mind and spirit.

Teaching Christians how to read the early fathers or how to understand ancient interpretations of the Bible or catechetical confessions has a long history. Throughout most of the Middle Ages, patristic texts were presented in very short clips, often in single statements that themselves came from compendia (a group of texts clumped around important themes). Collected works from a single author were rare and found only in well-to-do libraries. Scholars and students alike learned in bits and pieces from the writings of the early church. There were numerous reasons for this method of learning, the most obvious being that not until the fifteenth century did theologians begin to make a concerted effort to pull together writings that originated from one author and to distinguish the authentic works of a writer from spurious ones. Truly, one of the great benefits of the modern era has been the ability to read the works of an early father collected and in sequence and, therefore, in context. There is no hyperbole in saying that we are far better equipped today to study the works of the early church than the ancient Christians were.

Nevertheless, there is still a good reason for learning the ancients in small portions within thematically related or exegetical contexts: namely, it is easier to remember. A student is more likely to recall a small, poignant passage from a specific writer focused on, say, the Lord's Prayer or humility or the meaning of the Son's being "born" of the Father than thumbing through pages and pages of text. While learning the wisdom of past ages in excerpted form is hardly ideal, it holds some benefits for the beginner. That is the approach taken in this volume.

Under nine headings related to how the church's tradition and the church's Bible were interpreted and "translated" into doctrine, the reader will encounter portions of texts from a variety of patristic writers. This is by no means a comprehensive collection. Think of the texts chosen as those best exhibiting some of the important developments in Christian history. You are, in effect, being encouraged to "Come, taste and see." In tasting, you will discover a new thirst for the important things of faith and practice, but remember that you are only scratching the surface. You will want to go further, which means you will want to read works in their entirety. To facilitate this next step, a specially prepared bibliography appears at the end of this book. The early fathers will always remain "suspicious" to Protestants, or any Christian, until they are actually heard and read.

This collection of texts was originally conceived as a companion volume to *Evangelicals and Tradition: The Formative Influence of the Early Church* (Baker, 2005). I intended this anthology to illustrate the various interpretive arguments made in the monograph. However, the sourcebook may just as easily be used independently as an introduction to the primary sources. Either way, it will enable students and teachers to read the patristic authors directly, even if in excerpts, on issues related to the earliest developments of Scripture and tradition and how these were interpreted. In them lie the cornerstones of Christian authority for the church past and future.

DHW

Do you not know that those who run a race all run, but only one receives the prize? Run in such a way that you may win.

1 Corinthians 9:24

ABBREVIATIONS

ACW	Ancient Christian Writers
ANF	*The Ante-Nicene Fathers*, ed. A. Roberts and J. Donaldson, 10 vols. (1885–87; reprint, Grand Rapids: Eerdmans, 1979)
Butterworth, *Origen*	G. W. Butterworth, trans., *On First Principles: Being Koetschau's Text of the De principiis* (Gloucester, MA: Smith, 1973)
CCC	*Creeds, Councils and Controversies: Documents Illustrating the History of the Church, AD 337–461*, ed. J. Stevenson and W. H. C. Frend, rev. ed. (London: SPCK; 1989)
Connolly, *Explanatio*	R. H. Connolly, *The Explanatio symboli ad initiandos: A Work of St. Ambrose*, Texts and Studies 10 (Cambridge: Cambridge University Press, 1952)
Creeds and Confessions	*Creeds and Confessions of Faith in the Christian Tradition*, ed. Jaroslav Pelikan and Valerie Hotchkiss, 4 vols. (New Haven: Yale University Press, 2003)
CSCO	*Philoxenus of Mabbug: Fragments of the Commentary on Matthew and Luke*, trans. J. W. Watt, 2 vols. Corpus scriptorum christianorum orientalium 393 (Louvain: Corpusco, 1978)
FOC	Fathers of the Church (Washington, DC: Catholic University of America Press)
Froehlich, *Biblical Interpretation*	Karlfried Froehlich, trans. and ed., *Biblical Interpretation in the Early Church*, Sources of Early Christian Thought (Philadelphia: Fortress, 1984)
Green, *De doctrina christiana*	R. P. H. Green, ed. and trans., *De doctrina christiana: Augustine*, Oxford Early Christian Texts (Oxford: Clarendon, 1995)
Hanson, *Tradition*	R. P. C. Hanson, *Tradition in the Early Church* (London: SPCK, 1962)
HE	*Historia ecclesiastica* (Church History)

Holmes, *Apostolic Fathers*	Michael W. Holmes, ed. and rev., *The Apostolic Fathers: Greek Texts and English Translations*, updated ed. (Grand Rapids: Baker, 1999)
Kannengiesser, *Early Christian Spirituality*	Charles Kannengiesser, ed., *Early Christian Spirituality*, trans. Pamela Bright, Sources of Early Christian Thought (Philadelphia: Fortress, 1986)
Kelly, *Early Christian Creeds*	J. N. D. Kelly, *Early Christian Creeds*, 3rd ed. (London: Longman, 1972)
Lawlor and Oulton, *Ecclesiastical History*	H. J. Lawlor and J. E. L. Oulton, trans., *The Ecclesiastical History and the Martyrs of Palestine* (London: SPCK, 1954)
LCC 1	*Early Christian Fathers*, trans. C. C. Richardson, Library of Christian Classics 1 (Philadelphia: Westminster, 1953)
LCC 3	Edward Rochie Hardy, ed., *Christology of the Later Fathers*, Library of Christian Classics 3 (Philadelphia: Westminster, 1954)
LCC 4	*Cyril of Jerusalem and Nemesius of Emesa*, ed. W. Telfer, Library of Christian Classics 4 (Philadelphia: Westminster, 1954)
McCarthy, *Saint Ephrem's Commentary*	Carmel McCarthy, *Saint Ephrem's Commentary on Tatian's Diatessaron: An English Translation of Chester Beatty Syriac MS 709*, Journal of Semitic Studies: Supplement 2 (Oxford: Oxford University Press for the University of Manchester, 1993)
NPNF 1	*Nicene and Post-Nicene Fathers of the Christian Church*, series 1, ed. Philip Schaff, 14 vols. (1886–90; reprint, Grand Rapids: Eerdmans, 1983–87)
NPNF 2	*Nicene and Post-Nicene Fathers of the Christian Church*, series 2, ed. Philip Schaff and Henry Wace, 14 vols. (1890–1900; reprint, Grand Rapids: Eerdmans, 1983–87)
OTP	*The Old Testament Pseudepigrapha*, ed. James H. Charlesworth, 2 vols. (Garden City, NY: Doubleday, 1983–85)
PG	*Patrologiae cursus completus: Series graeca*, ed. J.-P. Migne, 161 vols. (Paris, 1857–86)
PL	*Patrologiae cursus completus: Series latina*, ed. J.-P. Migne, 221 vols. (Paris, 1844–64; 2nd ed., 1878–90)
SC	Sources chrétiennes (Paris: Cerf, 1943–)
Stevenson and Frend, *New Eusebius*	J. Stevenson and W. H. C. Frend, *A New Eusebius: Documents Illustrating the History of the Church to AD 337*, rev. ed. (London: SPCK, 1987)
Walpole, *Early Latin Hymns*	A. S. Walpole, trans., *Early Latin Hymns* (Cambridge: Cambridge University Press, 1922)
Williams, *Arius*	Rowan Williams, *Arius: Heresy and Tradition* (London: 1987; rev. ed., Eerdmans, 2001)
WSA	*The Works of Saint Augustine: A Translation for the Twenty-first Century*, trans. Edmund Hill, ed. John E. Rotelle (Brooklyn, NY: New City, 1990–2005)

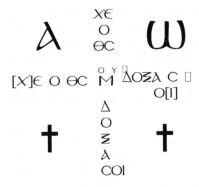

A personal prayer and doxology in the shape of a cross (anonymous, Tyre, fourth or fifth cent.). This Greek inscription appears on a marble plaque used to cover the opening of a loculus (recessed burial niche). Both horizontally and vertically, the text reads Χ[ΡΙΣΤ]Ε Ο Θ[ΕΟ]Σ ΜΟΥ ΔΟΞΑ ΣΟΙ ("Christ my God, glory to you"). The last word of the inscription is out of position to accommodate the dimensions of the plaque. An alpha and omega (the first and last letters of the Greek alphabet) and two crosses fill the squares formed by the cross-shaped inscription. We find in this text both a personal address to Christ and a liturgical allusion (from G. H. R. Horsley, ed., *New Documents Illustrating Early Christianity*, vol. 2 [North Ryde, NSW: Ancient History Documentary Research Centre, Macquarie University, 1982], 154).

INTRODUCTION

Patristic Background of Scripture and Tradition

> Be very careful, Christian friends, that no one of you be found not only
> not speaking with or reflecting wisdom, but even despising and opposing
> those who pursue the study of wisdom. The ignorant, among other prob-
> lems, have this worst fault of all: they consider those who have devoted
> themselves to the word and teaching as vain and useless. They prefer
> their own ignorance (which they call spiritual "simplicity") to the study
> and labors of the learned.
>
> (Origen of Alexandria, *Homily on Psalm 36*)

A S AN ANTHOLOGY of ancient Christian sources, this collection seeks to illustrate the ways in which the church's confessions, teaching, biblical interpretation, and worship were expressed
in the late first to the fifth centuries of the Christian era. This period,
known as the patristic age, or "age of the early fathers," is not merely
important for understanding church history, but it has also functioned
as a cornerstone of Christian identity for all later ages. The major creeds
such as the Nicene and the Apostles' creeds have been the most visible,
but we cannot neglect the lesser known yet just as significant theological
texts and confessions, interpretations, and hymnody that were seminal
in shaping the early Christian identity. For this reason, the well-known
and the not-so-well-known are represented in the readings below.

This volume is not meant to be a commentary on the various patristic
texts cited, though the reader will encounter a few scattered explanations for certain words, phrases and some historical background. The
intent, rather, is to provide a limited number of texts that illuminate
major themes related to the teaching of basic Christian truths, the early

tradition, the rise and form of the Christian Bible, and how the latter two were inextricably intertwined in the life of the church. As a result, the reader will be able to perceive something of the earliest stages of Christian doctrine, use of the Bible, and methods of interpretation.

Some Protestant readers may be suspicious of some subjects included in this book. Surely any discussion about authority in the early church has to do mainly with the Bible and its final canonization. And indeed, this work takes that development seriously, just as the early fathers did. Under the aegis of the Holy Spirit, the text of both the Old and New Testaments—sometimes simply referred to as "Prophet and Apostle"—was the primary agent of God's ongoing work of transformation in and through the church. There was no question in the patristic mind that Scripture (in its various Latin, Greek, Syriac, and other versions that existed) was the sourcebook for the wording of creeds, as well as the substance for explaining the faith. Whether it was a local baptismal confession or an "ecumenical" creed, the content had to reflect Scripture in its wording and convictions. Cyril of Jerusalem taught new believers that the creed (of Jerusalem) was *de facto* a summarization of the Scriptures. Indeed, one of the main purposes for learning the creed, he says, is because it represents an epitome of the whole Bible.

> Learn the faith and profess it; receive it and keep it—but only the Creed which the church will now deliver to you, that Creed is firmly based on Scripture. . . . For the articles of the Creed were not put together according to human choice; the most important doctrines were collected from the whole of Scripture to make up a single exposition of the faith.[1]

Because each article of the creed, as Cyril expounds them, is so thoroughly grounded in biblical authority, he insists that his hearers must not accept anything without reference to the sacred Scriptures: "Do not simply take my word when I tell you these things, unless you are given proof for my teaching from Holy Scripture."[2] Such sentiments were the norm for the patristic age. The fifth-century Syrian bishop, Philoxenus of Hierapolis (Mabbug), also makes this clear: "The truth, the accurate account, which is the lasting and steadfast, is revealed only by the revelation of God. If one should seek something outside of these things which are set down in Scripture, one cannot understand."[3]

And yet, the early fathers would not have understood, much less appreciated, the principle of Scripture alone (*sola scriptura*). In the first place, the historical and theological issues that gave rise to this doctrine

---

1. *Catechetical Lectures* 5.12; LCC 4:124.
2. Ibid., 4.17.
3. Frag. 28 (CSCO 393:28–29).

were peculiar to late medieval and Reformation-era Christianity.[4] More importantly, Irenaeus, Tertullian, Origen, Cyprian, and others were convinced that the authors of Scripture shared an agreement about the particulars of the church's tradition (called the Rule or Canon of Faith in the second and third centuries). They believed the "Rule" was the *ratio*, or what Athanasius calls the "scope," of scriptural revelation. Thus, to treat the Bible in isolation from the tradition of the church, as it was located in the ancient Rule of Faith, baptismal confessions, and conciliar creeds, would have been incomprehensible to the Christian pastors and thinkers of the patristic age. From their perspective, a radically biblicist view might easily be driven by a desire to *avoid* the truth of the church's teaching, as it seems to have been an issue in dealing with the Marcionites and Arians.[5] In any case, a principle of Scripture alone would not have secured an orthodox interpretation of Scripture, since it was obvious that various religious groups had used the Bible to teach almost anything. Precisely on this point Tertullian wrote:

> What sort of truth is that which they patronize, when they commend it to us with a lie? Well, they actually treat the Scriptures and recommend their opinions out of the Scriptures. To be sure they do![6]

The authority of the Bible was not in question, it was how the Bible should rightly be used, and which texts spoke authentically for the apostolic teaching.

Thus, the interpretation of the Bible, regarding it as a divinely inspired text, and even the very form that it took as a collection—both are indebted to factors outside the Bible. Though the word in Scripture comes from God, it is revealed through a process in which the earliest Christian churches were profoundly involved. In its final formation, the Bible came out of the life of the Christian community as it heard God's word and sought to realize it faithfully. What this means is that the Bible is foremost the book of the church and the church's history.[7]

---

4. The beginning of the end of a co-inherent understanding of Scripture and tradition (and the church) appears by the fourteenth century. George Tavard points to Henry Ghent's *Commentary on the Sentences*, written in the thirteenth century, which raised the question whether Christians are mandated to believe Scripture ("authorities of doctrine") rather than those of the church. Ghent supposes that if the church taught anything contrary to Scripture, the believer should believe not in the church but in the words of Christ. *Holy Writ or Holy Church* (London: Burns & Oates, 1959), 24–25.

5. For illustration, see D. H. Williams, "The Search for *Sola Scriptura* in the Early Church," *Interpretation* 52 (1998): 338–50.

6. *On the Prescription of Heretics* 15.

7. This is essentially the thesis behind a new series of patristic commentary on Scripture titled The Church's Bible, ed. Robert L. Wilken (Grand Rapids: Eerdmans, 2003–).

One would think that the oft-cited admonition of 2 Pet. 1:20 would be taken literally as condemning the privatization of biblical interpretation and application: "Above all, you must understand that no prophecy of Scripture came about by the prophet's own interpretation." Many Christians, however, claim this passage to prove the divine character of Scripture. Of course God works in a single human heart, but the chief task of interpretation and realization of Scripture as a defined compilation was an ongoing ecclesiological event, with the result that the church and its tradition are integral to the handling of the Bible and its canonization.

But let us be clear about what this last statement is *not* saying. It is not opposed to the principle of soul liberty as long as soul liberty does not itself become a canon of faith, supposedly guaranteeing religious freedom above all else. Unfortunately, the protective aspect of soul freedom as a bulwark against any form of church authority or confessionalism has been, and still is, exaggerated to the distortion of hyper-individualism and privatization of religious faith. The paranoia among anti-fundamentalists[8] is so strong that any kind of Christianity that sounds creedal or liturgical or advocates doctrinal standards tends to be rejected as incongruent with personal freedom in Christ. However (and fortunately), this problem pertains more to contemporary church politics than to the apostolic and patristic concepts of authority. In Paul's marvelous address, we read about the believer being set free from sin for the work of grace:

> But thanks be to God that, though you used to be slaves to sin, you wholeheartedly obeyed the form of teaching to which you were entrusted. (Rom. 6:17)

The "form of teaching" is some body of doctrinal and moral precepts of the apostolic preaching to which believers were required to adhere (cf. 1 Cor. 15:1–3). Casting off ecclesial standards of doctrine and morality as if they lead to authoritarianism misses the point entirely. Obedience to "the form of teaching" was the way to freedom!

We must also observe that the integral association of Scripture, tradition, and church does not necessitate the squelching of the Spirit. It seems to be a general axiom in evangelical religious circles that spiritual freedom is the opposite of adopting a prescribed standard of beliefs and practices; charismatic is the exact opposite of creed. But notice, for the apostle Paul, one of the main architects of the church's tradition,

---

8. "Fundamentalism" is a problematic term because its alleged associations are too broad, unless we are using it in reference to a particular history or an identifiable group.

how the pneumatic, charismatic character of early Christianity never excluded the authority of the church's confessions and teaching. The Christian was set free henceforth to "walk in the Spirit," but it was understood that the Christian walked within the context of a specific and articulated faith that was transmitted for the congregation to preserve. So Paul writes:

> What you heard from me, keep as a pattern of sound teaching, with faith and love in Christ Jesus. Guard the good deposit that was entrusted to you—guard it with the help of the Holy Spirit who lives in us. (2 Tim. 1:13–14)

Therefore, it is important that the reader recognize the principles of freedom from the law and Spirit-led faith were never meant to be taken in isolation from the consensual and foundational tradition of the church. Like streams coming out of the same spring, the tradition and the Bible, represented by the work of the Holy Spirit in the church, *were realized only in the presence of each other.*

Let's take a more detailed look at the emergence of the earliest tradition as well as some examples for how these "streams" first emerged and took particular shape. Since "tradition" seems the least understood and the most mistrusted among many Protestant readers, we'll deal with that first, and then show how Scripture and the tradition were woven together from the beginning of the Christian church.

The Preaching, or Tradition, of the Apostles

From the earliest stages of the Christian church, the language of "tradition" was the primary means of expressing the transmission of apostles' teaching, which was itself reflective of the Lord's own proclamation. The apostle Paul encouraged the Thessalonians to "stand firm and hold to the traditions we passed on to you" (2 Thess. 2:15). By "traditions"[9] the apostle is using the word in its usual sense; a process of handing over and receiving something, in this case, a living and active transmission of the church's preaching. In this instance, his emphasis appears to be on ethical tradition, on corporate and personal Christian practices.[10]

Most importantly, not only does Paul *not* set these "traditions" and his writing in opposition to one another; he also sees them as entirely

9. Greek, *paradoseis*. Most unfortunately, the NIV Bible translates this word as "teachings."

10. For a parallel, see Col. 2:6: "Just as you have received [*paralambanō*] Christ Jesus as Lord, continue to live in him."

complementary, just as the remaining part of the verse reads: "Hold to the traditions we passed on to you, whether by mouth or by letter." His letter to the church was meant to confirm what traditions the readers had already been teaching. As such, Paul commands his readers to avoid any brother who "does not live according to the tradition (*paradosis*) you received (*paralambanō*) from us" (2 Thess. 3:6). Both the noun and the verb of tradition(al) language is being used here, in all likelihood, to stress that those who do not accept Paul's teaching are opposing not merely him, but also the teaching of the whole church.

The same was true for his letter to the Corinthian church. By the time he wrote 1 Corinthians (ca. AD 57), the church already possessed a normative standard (the *paradosis*) (1 Cor. 11:2) of the "what" and "how" of the Christian faith. Using the vibrant language of tradition, Paul says he himself "received" (*paralambanō*) this "Gospel" from the Lord, with which he also "delivered" (*paradidōmi*) to his readers (1 Cor. 11:23; 15:3). This language is meant to stress the interactive nature of the tradition, rather like a football play: at the signal, the center hikes the ball, the quarterback receives it, and then he passes or hands it off to another player, who then receives it. The entire event, or "play," is dynamic. This was no less true of the apostolic proclamation of Christ whose "play" of tradition occurred in living communities by way of prayer, preaching, singing, baptizing, and celebrating the Lord's Supper.

What is called tradition in 1 Cor. 11 had to do with order of worship, specifically, celebrating the Lord's Supper. In 1 Cor. 15, the tradition "of first importance" was a doctrinal one that enabled the Christians to interpret the Old Testament: "that Christ died for our sins according to the Scriptures; that he was buried, that he was raised on the third day according to the Scriptures, and that he appeared to Peter, and then to the Twelve" (vv. 3–5). Again, there is no perceived conflict between what the Corinthians had received by way of the church's existing tradition and the epistle which would become "Scripture."

In Paul's statements, there also is no tension between the gospel as revelation and the gospel as tradition. Revelation and the tradition were but two sides of one coin.[11] Thus, the tradition did not stand against the inspirational process out of which emerged the New Testament; it was a critical means by which the risen Lord had imparted his revelation through the working of the Spirit.

There are several general ways to understand the tradition as it first appears and begins to mature into different and more sophisticated forms. The Christian tradition was (and to a certain extent still is) in a process of development, which meant that changes were inevitable.

11. F. F. Bruce, *Tradition: Old and New* (Grand Rapids: Zondervan, 1970), 31–32.

Since the transmission of faith is, at all levels, tied up with time, language, and culture, there is always change, and change is inherently imperfect, always subject to reformation. In this process the tradition was responding to the church's present circumstances in light of its past. Development, therefore, was not change for its own sake but the result of discovering how the deposit of faith should function as a resource for the needs of the present.

Another way to think of the ancient tradition is that it functions as the memory of the church. If tradition is a preserver of the church's faith as the work of God in the body of Christ, then it is supposed to be a living and shared memory. In this sense, we are being directed to the role of the church, which harbors the tradition and is also the agent for handing the tradition over to new believers and to the world. Tradition as memory is not the work of the individual believer, although the believer participates in it, but of the corporate body of Christ, the church. Only within the church can memory reside each time the Lord's Supper is observed or a new Christian is baptized, where the memory of the faith is called back and re-experienced. As memory, tradition has to do with how the gospel is transmitted, how the divine presence is realized in the sacraments (or ordinances) among believers, and how lives are changed by Christian truth.

Defining the Canon

Many readers have been taught that the "canon" refers to the accepted list of biblical books in the Old and New Testaments. In general, however, the meaning of "canon" refers to any mechanism for standardizing a measurement or an evaluation. Speaking in a Christian context, the "canon" is a fixed norm or rule for determining the parameters of Christian thought and life. In Gal. 6:15–16, the apostle Paul closes his letter to the Galatians, reminding them that when it comes to the cross of Christ, "neither circumcision nor uncircumcision means anything." What matters is how Jew and Gentile can be made a "new creation" according to redemption that comes through Christ. Rather than measuring oneself by the law of circumcision, Paul says, peace and mercy are upon those who follow "this canon."[12] The mention of canon here has nothing to do with a list of authoritative texts; rather, it refers to a standard or rule of belief and living. In chapter 2, Paul may be alluding to an earlier reference of this same canon when he complains about those Jews at Antioch who have separated themselves from the Gentiles

12. The NIV translates the word "canon" as "rule."

and thus are not acting in line "with the truth of the gospel" (Gal. 2:14). Elsewhere, Paul speaks of an existing standard of faith that correlates with his message of the Christian faith. Best known is his outline of the "tradition" in 1 Cor. 15:2–8:

> that Christ died for our sins, . . .
> that he was buried,
> that he was raised on the third day . . .

Paul says this threefold litany of events has happened in accordance with the ancient prophets and was witnessed by the apostles. Further examples of Paul's use of the earliest tradition are found in chapter 8.A, below.

The most familiar way to render "canon" is by referring to the fixing of authoritative religious texts into a standardized body (as for the New Testament). And so the term is commonly used for those books of Scripture that the church has recognized to be divinely inspired and therefore authoritative for Christian faith and practice. We have seen, however, that the term "canon" has nothing necessarily to do with a list(s) of texts. There was transmission of the Christian faith *before* it was rendered into text as a letter or narrative, and well before there was any kind of codification of Christian texts. Although there is no one structure or content in the earliest stages of the apostolic message, we do find a set of recurring themes based on the revelation of God in Christ as seen through his incarnate life, servanthood through his crucifixion, death, burial, and the remaking of creation from his resurrection and lordship. There was indeed a sense of a "canon" or standard of teaching (see chap. 4, below) having to do with standard features of the apostles' preaching. Both narratives and texts were often acknowledged to be authoritative within Christian churches before they were placed, if ever, into fixed and standardized formats.

What is not so commonly understood is that, while the New Testament was written by apostles and the earliest followers of Christ in the first century, its formation into a concrete and recognized collection, along with the Old Testament,[13] is a uniquely patristic accomplishment. The formal means by which the biblical books were regarded as divinely given, and therefore sharing equal authority with the Hebrew Scripture, took

---

13. Not till the end of the second century was the phrase "Old Testament" used as a way of distinguishing it from the "Gospel and Apostle." The earliest known usage is in the *Book of Extracts* of Melito of Sardis, a document quoted by Eusebius of Caesarea (*HE* 4.26.12) and known only in fragmentary form. There was no exact agreement on the parameters of the content of the Old Testament, as a comparison with Melito's list and the Masoretic text shows.

place in the postapostolic centuries of the early church (2nd–4th cent.). This process was a gradual and untidy one, which emerged out of the worship and confessional practices of the early churches. Nevertheless, the very concept of "canon" was first applied to the church's profession of faith, not to a list of authoritative texts. What the church *believed* was canonical prior to that belief taking written, codified forms. In effect, the earliest "canons" or norms of the preaching and defending of the early tradition served as the standard for the canonization of texts.

Canonical Authority

Simply put, the faith articulated during the first five centuries set into place two pillars of authority on which Christians have stood: an *apostolic canon of Scripture* (the Bible), and a *theological canon of apostolicity* (cardinal doctrines and confessions of the Trinity, Christology, etc.). The first has to do with the process of codifying the collection of the New Testament, and that is not complete without the Old Testament. In other words, Gospel and Apostle are never supposed to function severed from the Prophets. Jesus's words to the disciples along the Emmaus road in Luke 24 serve as the archetype for this axiom. The second, a theological canon of apostolicity, refers to the forms in which the early church laid down the baseline of essential Christian truths: confessions, creeds, doctrines, interpretations of the Bible, hymns, and so on. Scripture, as the written and fixed authority, eventually becomes the "primary canon," or what some scholars have called the formal canon, while the tradition, or the functional canon, is the guide or rule, possessing fixed and fluid forms that are both oral and written. Although the New Testament, along with the Old Testament, will become the *norma normans* (norm that sets the norm), the historical fact is that the apostolic tradition is as primitive as the Christian Scripture. The scriptural canon came about in its shape and content as an embodiment of the canonical tradition, and this tradition could only be legitimated by standing in unity with the teaching of Scripture.

Does the above mean that Scripture is subservient to tradition? The very wording of this question is built on an assumption that Scripture and tradition must lie in antithesis to one another. This is a particularly Protestant worry, one that has influenced and shaped post-sixteenth-century theology to a wide and unfortunate extent. As I said earlier, early Christians would have been baffled by framing Scripture and tradition in this way. The ancient fathers themselves taught that the tradition was the epitome of the Christian faith, the very purport of

Scripture. All the major creeds and works of theology acknowledged, implicitly or explicitly, the supremacy of the Bible.

Patristic Tradition as Canon

For almost two millennia, the church's tradition has functioned by providing Christians with the essential baseline of theological faithfulness. But it has not always been clear which elements of the tradition should serve as ongoing standards for Christianity and which are denominationally or culturally specific. Since the sixteenth century, one of the persistent conflicts between Protestants, Roman Catholics, and the Greek Orthodox involves discerning which aspects of traditions are normative and which are not.

The tradition that originated in the apostolic and postapostolic centuries does not offer a monolithic picture of the church, but it does supply the theological and confessional building blocks upon which ensuing Christian thought, practice, and worship have been built. While the tradition may not be reduced to the early church, it certainly includes it and is largely defined by it. As such, the tradition is the various incarnations of the Christian faith articulated during the first five or six centuries.[14] In real and tangible ways, this period has functioned like a "canon" of Christian theology (doctrine, liturgy, prayer, exegesis, etc.) and has been the basis for directing the course of subsequent theology over the last millennium and a half. In other words, the apostolic and patristic legacies are foundational to the Christian faith in *normative* ways that no other period of the church's history can claim. A theologian or pastor may agree or disagree with aspects of the patristic legacy, but it functions nonetheless as a rule by which such agreement or disagreement occurs. Even from a postmodern orientation, which refuses to identify with any standards of faith as enduring standards, all theologizing is still done using a terminology and conceptuality that

14. Different scholars place the end of the patristic era between the fifth and the seventh centuries, and there is no agreement on this because there is no one definitive event or author that marks the end. The best way to indicate the close of the "age of the fathers" is when writers begin to look backward in time for religious authority rather than to the present to validate their arguments. While the ancient Christians always regarded the past with high esteem, one can point to an increasing amount of instances in the late fifth and six centuries when writers thought of the earlier "fathers" as privileged witnesses to Christian truth. This is, like all alternatives, quite subjective, and exceptions to it can be found. It does more justice, however, to the nuances required for the various factors of historical interpretation. See Patrick Gray, "'The Select Fathers': Canonizing the Patristic Past," *Studia patristica* 23 (1989): 21–36.

is beholden to established norms of the Christian past and shapes the direction of the future.[15]

The most familiar example of the patristic age as canon is how the Apostles' Creed and the Nicene-Constantinopolitan Creed have remained theological and ecclesiastical guideposts for signaling the way of orthodoxy for the Christian faith. Even for those church communions that do not regularly profess these creeds or acknowledge them in worship, the faith of these churches is dependent upon the theology that the major creeds represent. The raw material for such teaching may be from the New Testament, but the doctrines about Christ as true God and true man and about God as Trinity and the relationship between Creator and the creation were formulated and established in the patristic age.

As for the great creeds of the early church (see chap. 5, below), especially the Nicene, they came to function "canonically" when they were communicated, not merely in the literal terms of the creed itself, but also as their later interpretations lifted them out from among all other creeds and made them normative.[16] In the later reception of Nicaea, we see that it was just as important to configure the meaning of the creed as it was to recount its words. Reminiscent of the fixed fluidity of the Rule(s) of Faith of earlier centuries, the Christian leaders at Alexandria (362), Constantinople (381), and Chalcedon (451) all defer to the Nicene Creed (325) as foundational, though they did not believe that the way of doctrinal faithfulness lay in the literal reproduction of the creed.[17] In fact, it took the theological developments of a "neo-Nicene" interpretation of the creed in order for the creed to come back into general acceptance and circulation within the churches.

Beyond Chalcedon, later church councils and theologians point to the Nicene Creed as the beginning point for establishing orthodoxy, as well as the councils of Constantinople (381), Ephesus (431), and Chalcedon (451). No matter how many more "ecumenical councils" one accepts, whether a total of seven with the Eastern Orthodox,[18] or twenty-one with Roman Catholicism,[19] or whether other important but not "ecumenical"

15. See Lieven Boeve, *Interrupting Tradition: An Essay on Christian Faith in a Postmodern Context* (Grand Rapids: Eerdmans, 2003).

16. Michel René Barnes, "The Fourth Century as Trinitarian Canon," in *Christian Origins: Theology, Rhetoric, and Community*, ed. Lewis Ayres (New York: Routledge, 1998), 62.

17. Anne-Michèle de Halleux, "La réception du symbole oecuménique de Nicée à Chalcédoine," *Ephemerides theologicae lovanienses* 61 (1985): 25.

18. In addition to the first four, Constantinople II (553), Constantinople III (680), and Nicaea II (787) are designated as "ecumenical" because they were supposedly councils of the undivided church. These seven stand as the formal deposit of normative teaching for Eastern Orthodoxy.

19. C. J. Hefele, *A History of the Christian Councils* (Edinburgh: T&T Clark, 1894), 63–64.

councils should also figure as authoritative sources for doctrine[20]—none of these share the same foundational character as Nicaea and the patristic creeds of the fourth and fifth centuries. So Gregory of Rome ("the Great"), declares in one of his many preserved letters:

> I receive and revere as the four books of the gospel so also the four councils, that is, the Nicene, Constantinopolitan, Ephesine, and Chalcedonian, . . . since on them, as on a four-square stone, rises the structure of the holy faith.[21]

While Gregory admits that he also accepts other later councils, it is upon the four first councils, "having been constituted by universal consent," that the norms for Christian faith and life reside. The so-called fifth ecumenical council (Constantinople II in 553) "set its seal to the creed that was put forth by the 318 [Nicene] Fathers and again piously confirmed by the 150 [at Constantinople, 381], which also other holy synods received and ratified." A similar affirmation is made by the (so-called) sixth and seventh ecumenical councils. The seventh, the council of Nicaea II (787), makes it clear that the Nicene Creed is preeminent among the later ecumenical synods. Unto the present day, then, the Nicene Creed is the statement par excellence of what the Christian church believes, as one finds in the liturgies of Roman Catholicism, Anglicanism, Eastern Orthodoxy, and various Protestant orders of service. Along with the Apostles' Creed, the Nicene Creed has been the heart of ecumenical confessionalism, and it is the basis on which nearly all Christian communions can agree.[22]

Reading Scripture by the Tradition

No matter what theory of biblical inspiration was held, the practice of reading and hearing Scripture in the ancient church did not occur without the tradition. An anonymous writer at the end of the first century addresses the church at Corinth in order to encourage believers to avoid worldly practices and seek heartfelt repentance. Central to this exhortation, the church leaders are told therefore to embrace "the glorious and holy canon of our tradition."[23] Here and elsewhere the writer

20. E.g., Serdica (or Sardica, modern Sophia, Bulgaria, in 342/43), Carthage (397), Toledo (400).

21. *Epistle* 25.

22. Hans-Georg Link, ed., *The Roots of Our Common Faith: Faith in the Scriptures and in the Early Church* (Geneva: World Council of Churches, 1984); M. Heim, ed., *Faith to Creed: Ecumenical Perspectives on the Affirmation of the Apostolic Faith in the Fourth Century* (Grand Rapids: Eerdmans, 1991); Frederick Norris, *The Apostolic Faith: Protestants and Roman Catholics* (Collegeville, MN: Liturgical Press, 1992).

23. See *1 Clement* 7.2–4.

displays no cognizance of an operational scriptural canon apart from the Old Testament, which he frequently cites as declaring fully and unambiguously the gospel of Jesus Christ. Implicit to the writer's argument is that one obtains an apostolic understanding only when Scripture is read through the lenses of the "canon of our tradition." Through these "lenses" a spiritual interpretation can be regarded as viable.

Doctrinal historians have referred to this symbiotic relationship between Scripture and the tradition as "co-inherence" (or "coincidence"),[24] since the content of the church's confessional tradition coinhered with the content of Scripture. The patristic mind comprehended tradition and Scripture in reciprocal terms. While Scripture had the primacy of place for the fathers, they did not believe that Scripture could or should function in the life of the believer apart from the church's traditional teaching and language of worship. Scripture was the authoritative anchor of tradition's content, and tradition stood as the primary interpreter of Scripture. In other words, the tradition was not a novel set of beliefs and practices made as an addition to Scripture, as if it were a separate and second revelatory source. In this vein, Thomas Aquinas asserted that the value of the biblical writers should not be separated from the early fathers, since the latter are the reliable interpreters of Scripture and the organs that continue the tradition.[25] Taken in this way, tradition is also an approach for interpreting the Bible by investigating and following the ancient consensus of the fathers. Their resulting theology accurately represented the message of Scripture.

It is the tradition or apostolic preaching that formed the basis of the New Testament and served as the hermeneutical model for interpreting the Old Testament. As the body of this tradition developed over the next three to four centuries, it was understood as that which bears witness to and interprets Scripture. Whether it was the baptismal formulas, catechetical summaries, or the later creeds, these all were valued as accurately representing the purport of Scripture. When instructing new converts, Augustine taught, "For whatever you hear in the Creed is contained in the inspired books of Holy Scripture."[26] To describe the tradition was inevitably to speak about the message of Scripture.

24. A. N. S. Lane, "Scripture, Tradition and Church: An Historical Survey," *Vox evangelica* 9 (1975): 37–55; Richard Bauckham, "Tradition in Relation to Scripture and Reason," in *Scripture, Tradition and Reason: A Study in the Criteria of Christian Doctrine*, ed. R. Bauckham and B. Dewey (Edinburgh: T&T Clark, 1988), 117–45.

25. John Henry Newman, in the preface to Thomas Aquinas, *Catena aurea: Commentary on the Four Gospels Collected out of the Works of the Fathers* (Oxford: J. H. Parker, 1841), 1:vii.

26. *Sermon* 212.2.

Though a century apart from one another, Vincent of Lérins and Gregory of Rome ("the Great") articulated a structure of authority that was already acknowledged as a standard. Orthodox (or catholic) Christianity could be shown in two ways: "first, by the authority of the divine canon (the Bible), and the other by the tradition of the catholic church." The authority of the first outweighed the authority of the second: Vincent claimed that the canon [of Scripture] suffices alone on any matter. But he acknowledged the fact that the Bible cannot function in isolation from the early church's tradition lest it fall prey to faulty interpretations. A rule of faith or norm for interpretation is essential if orthodox faith is to be achieved. "It is therefore necessary that the interpretation of divine Scripture should be ruled according to the one standard of the church's belief, especially in those articles on which the foundations of all catholic doctrine rest."[27]

The Bible as Canon

How the particular books of the Bible became a standardized list or collection for the church has been the subject of a great many studies.[28] For this reason, we need only deal with the subject briefly. One thing becomes clear in a study on the patristic concept of canonization of Scripture: the early church wasn't as concerned with establishing an authorized list of books of the Bible as modern historians have assumed. There was no one council or primal document that "decided" which books should be in the Old and New Testaments, or rather, which ones should not. No one writer or sequence of writers determined the shape of the biblical canon. The truth is that the process was much less neat and categorical than we may like because (1) no one was in a hurry to decide the limits of Scripture.[29] On the whole, the earliest Christians did not trouble themselves about the criteria of canonicity of texts, as

27. *Commonitorium* 1.29, 76. This part is really the end of the second book of the *Commonitorium*, the first part being lost.

28. Some of the more reliable ones are W. R. Farmer and D. M. Farkasfalvy, *The Formation of the NT Canon* (Ramsey, NJ: Paulist Press, 1983); F. F. Bruce, *The Canon of Scripture* (Downers Grove, IL: InterVarsity, 1988); Bruce M. Metzger, *The Canon of the New Testament* (Oxford: Clarendon, 1987); L. McDonald, *The Formation of the Christian Biblical Canon*, rev. ed. (Peabody, MA: Hendrickson, 1995).

29. Marcion's insistence (middle 2nd cent.) that only the Pauline Epistles and an expurgated version of Luke's Gospel presented true Christianity has been overinterpreted to mean that Marcion's efforts in identifying a scriptural canon thereby instigated the early church to do likewise. Despite the prevalent theory that Marcion prompted, at least indirectly, the growth of the biblical canon, there was no second- or third-century writer who responded to Marcion's views with a fixed canon of books. The same problem is true

F. F. Bruce once commented; and (2) apart from a "core" of texts, the recognition of a complete collection of Scripture varied from West to East and even from region to region.

The Hebrew Bible, or Old Testament, was largely determined by the time of Jesus. It was automatic for the first disciples of the risen Christ to regard these texts as given by God and the basis for understanding the life and purpose of Christ, just as Peter's sermon in Acts 2 demonstrates. The Bible that Christians used was the Septuagint, a Greek version of the Hebrew translated by Jews for their predominantly Greek-speaking communities around the second century BC. The Septuagint (or close versions thereof) remained the authoritative version,[30] including its Latin translations, until the later fifth century.[31] Not until Jerome's translation of the Old Testament were Hebrew manuscripts consulted for revising the Latin Bible, and even then, Christians preferred the "tried and true" Septuagint. It was rather like the disputes that still occur today over the authority of the King James Bible (the Authorized Version of 1611) versus other more recent translations that have had the clear advantage of more and earlier manuscripts than when the King James version was published. Yet there are not a few Christians and churches that stand only on the authority of the King James Bible as the "Word of God." Long-standing attitudes of reverence toward one thing do not easily pass to another.

When it came to Christian texts, the primary issue on the minds of early believers was inspiration, not canonization. There was no postulated theory on the subject, but Christian interests followed the Jewish attitude toward the Hebrew Bible. Creating an exclusive list of authoritative books wasn't as important as making determinations between inspired and not inspired texts. Hence, one could refer to a particular writing as "Scripture" without wondering whether it was "canonical."[32] The prophets were enabled by the Spirit and spoke, "thus says the Lord," or as in the case of Moses and the seventy elders, "when the Spirit rested on them,

---

in attributing the "closing of the canon" to the Montanists and to their claim of ongoing revelation.

30. For the reason behind the Septuagint's divinely ordained status, see chap. 9.E, below.

31. There was great resistance on the part of the fourth-century Christians to the displacement of the Septuagint in favor of the more accurate translation from the Hebrew. Augustine's attitude was typical when he referred to the authority of the Septuagint as "supreme" and refused to allow its emendation or substitution as Jerome's Vulgate proposed to do "even if we find in the Hebrew versions something that differs from what they wrote" (*On Christian Teaching* 2.15.22; Green, *De doctrina christiana*, 81).

32. The distinction Bruce Metzger makes between "Scripture" and "canon" is helpful. There is a difference between a collection of authoritative books and an authoritative collection of books (*Canon of the New Testament*), 282.

they prophesied" (Num. 11:25). Paul too made it clear that "all Scripture [lit., 'every writing'] is God-breathed" (2 Tim. 3:16), certainly a reference to the Hebrew Bible. In this instance Paul is verifying the authority of the individual texts rather than referring to texts as a collection: he is not setting up a canon. Nevertheless, when it came to words and deeds of Jesus as recounted in the Gospels and many apostolic letters, there had not been much doubt about their divine inspiration. But by the middle of the second century, a growing number of other texts were regarded by many churches as inspired, such as the *Epistle of Barnabas* or *1 Clement* and a rather puzzling apocalyptic work known as the *Shepherd of Hermas*, which enjoyed widespread acceptance. These and others appear in some collections of biblical books by the fourth century, but not all were read in every church (as Scripture in worship). The book of Revelation was not regarded as inspired in some quarters, nor 2 Peter, James, or Hebrews; nevertheless, some collections included the Apocalypse of John, a manifestly apocryphal work. And in some cases, a text (such as the *Gospel of Matthias* or the *Gospel of Peter*) might be regarded as inspired and was read in the churches for edification, though it not did speak with the same authority as the Gospels or apostolic Epistles (see chap. 9.D, below). The so-called *Gospel of Judas* would have fallen into the same camp.[33]

The shape and content of the biblical canon, just like the theological canon, was formed as texts were received, used over time, and consistently affirmed as Scripture by the individual churches and their leaders. It may be disconcerting to learn just how subjective and uncharted the "canonical" process progressed from the end of the first century to the fourth century, apart from a few general guiding principles such

---

33. Despite the commotion caused by the fragments of the so-called *Gospel of Judas Iscariot*, second- and third-century gospels bearing apostolic names were quite numerous and, in some cases, were regarded as part of the scriptural writings. That there should be an apocryphal text purporting to be about Judas Iscariot, painting him in a slightly different light than do the four canonical Gospels, is not as surprising as it may at first seem. Popular early church stories tended to rehabilitate or humble those who were opposed to the historical Jesus. The *Acts of Pilate*, also known in various ancient versions as the *Gospel of Nicodemus*, tells of how Pilate himself became an advocate for Christ's miracles and just life. The soldiers who stood around the cross came to recognize Jesus's true identity. Nero's wife believed in Jesus in the *Acts of Peter and Paul*; the high priest Ananias is healed of blindness by the risen Christ (*Acts of Philip*). A number of accounts can be found of the previous lives of the two thieves who hung on crosses next to Jesus. The one who repented, later named Gestus, is said to have been the same robber who accosted the holy family on their way to Egypt but refused to let his companions steal any of their belongings (*Acts of Joseph*). Even Hades itself (in personified form) became fearful of Christ's descent into hell (Greek version of the *Gospel of Nicodemus*) and admits to Satan that his power has been conquered by Christ's presence.

as apostolicity, antiquity, and content in harmony with the tradition.[34] Only slowly did the church's interpretation of "Scripture" and canon meld into a single entity that entailed an exclusive (closed) collection of inspired books.[35]

Except perhaps for the canon in the "Muratorian Fragment" (see chap. 9.A, below), Eusebius of Caesarea at the end of the third century is the earliest source for providing a catalogue of biblical books that are accepted in his day. He is acquainted with the term "canon,"[36] but it is not his preferred terminology, likely because there was no one fixed body of biblical books by the late third and early fourth century. His narration is built around which books are the "acknowledged writings," those that are disputed, and those that are spurious. He is keenly interested to report how illustrious thinkers in the church's history used the Scriptures and which ones they used. For Eusebius, the undisputed biblical books are authoritative because they are "recognized by the churches under heaven" (3.24.2), and as such, these writings are those "acknowledged" by the churches. Several times Eusebius summarizes the books of the Old Testament. Only once does he itemize the writings of the New Testament (3.25.1–7), explaining that only the four Gospels, Acts, the Epistles of Paul, one of Peter and one of John, and perhaps Revelation, are among the "acknowledged" texts. Again, it appears that "disputed books" were nevertheless read in many churches, as were the spurious ones.

About seventy years later, Augustine enumerates a list of scriptural books accepted in the west in *On Christian Teaching*, a theological handbook for fellow pastors on interpreting the Bible. Typical of patristic authors, Augustine sees the Bible as a completely divine product; every sentence and possible meaning are intended by the Spirit's inspiration. Augustine's attempt to nail down an official list of books is indicative of a situation that lacked a single list because there was no one authoritative version of the Bible. Indeed, Augustine tells the reader that when it comes to determining the authoritative list of books, one should follow the lead of as many catholic churches as possible. In the case of those

34. Serapion of Antioch complained that the *Gospel of Peter* was being read (as Scripture) in the worship services of some churches (Eusebius, *HE* 6.12). The problem was that the text supports ideas unacceptable for an orthodox view of Jesus Christ as portrayed in the Gospels. Serapion declares that the ultimate rejection of the heretical gospel was not because it was missing in lists of scriptural books but because it violated the traditional faith of the (Antiochene) church.

35. See John Barton's helpful discussion on this matter in *Holy Writings, Sacred Text: The Canon in Christianity* (Louisville: Westminster/John Knox, 1997), esp. chaps. 1 and 5.

36. Eusebius states (*HE* 3.9.5) that Josephus gave the "number of the canonical writings in the Old Testament" (*Reply to Apion* 1.8). The term "canonical" is Eusebian, not from Josephus. The phrase "canon of the church" is used of Origen's knowledge of the extent of the biblical books (*HE* 6.25.3).

books not universally accepted, one should prefer those received by a majority of churches. This did not mean that the collection of Scripture as known to Augustine was not canonical. Several times Augustine calls the Scriptures canonical or the canon.[37] What he calls the "authoritative Old Testament" contained forty-four books, following the Septuagint version as always, and is reflected today in the Roman Catholic Bible. There seemed to be less controversy over the boundaries of the "authoritative New Testament," which squares with versions of the Bible today, though there still seemed to be serious questions raised about certain books.

Scripture as Divine Mystery

To the modern religious mind, perhaps the most foreign side of the fathers is in the area of biblical interpretation. Reading a creed or a letter from the patristic period is one thing, but trying to comprehend the reasoning behind vast tracts of commentary on Scripture can be bewildering. Our confusion has to do primarily with our inability to know how early writers "do" interpretation, which means we often have trouble following their train of thought. So in order to appreciate some of the mechanics behind the early church's understanding of Scripture, allow me to make brief observations on the ancients' approach to the Bible as a divine text. The readings incorporated in this volume will make this clearer. At least, we will see two operations at work in the patristic use of Scripture: (1) the divine and mystical character of Scripture in its very words, and (2) because of its divine nature, Scripture itself aids in the believer's transformation.

For many Protestants, the most problematic side to patristic use of the Bible is the fathers' predilection toward allegorical and spiritual interpretation of the text. Of the few problems Luther had with the early church, its allegorizing of the Bible was the biggest obstacle to sound scriptural understanding. He especially objected to the works of Origen, who justified allegory as the exegesis of the mature and faithful believer. The imaginative interpretation of Scripture permitted by allegorical method also led to its haphazard use in defense of seemingly fanciful speculations, for which Origen had a reputation. In Luther's eyes, the Holy Spirit is the simplest writer and adviser: "That is why his words [Scripture] could have no more than one simplest meaning which we call the written one or the literal meaning of the tongue."[38] Source and

37. *On Christian Teaching* 2.8.12–13.
38. Martin Luther, *Concerning the Letter and the Spirit*, in *Martin Luther: Selections from His Writings*, ed. J. Dillenberger (New York: Anchor, 1961), 78.

textual critical methods of exegesis that emerged from the biblical studies of late nineteenth and twentieth centuries were built upon normalizing of the reformer's penchant for the historical and literal interpretation.

But for ancient Christian thinkers, many biblical passages had more than one meaning precisely because Scripture was inspired by the Holy Spirit. On one hand, they took Scripture in quite literal terms, stressing the literality of Scripture such that each word and sentence had to be taken just as it was. As a generalization, it is fair to say that the fathers affirm an infallible Bible, although it is not an infallibility of the text as much as the infallibility of the divine intention behind the text. On the other hand, looking for a purely literal or historical approach in the Gospel text as the preferred interpretation was not something patristic writers valued as doing full justice to the sacred nature of Scripture. Quite the reverse: they claimed that points of obscurity or even contradiction within the Bible provided an opportunity for the Spirit to work in a Christian heart because the dilemma was more than the human mind could comprehend. So Origen states that divine providence is not voided when some do not accept the reality of conflicting accounts between scriptural writers[39] or morally questionable issues:[40] "The divine character of Scripture, which extends through all of it, is not abolished because our weakness cannot discern in every sentence the hidden splendor of its teachings."[41] Such problems were not obstacles to be overcome by manipulating the words, declaring that the text was interpolated, or wondering what the original autographs might have said. Rather, they were seen as open doors by which only the faithful could discover the power of God in ways not obvious to the unconverted or a carnal believer. Augustine, for example, explained in one of his sermons that obscure or conflicting passages in Scripture exist, not because God wants to conceal his mysteries from us, but "because he only wants to open them up to those who are prepared to look for them." Such texts are meant "to spur us on, heart and soul, to the search."[42] This is what Jesus meant, Augustine asserted, when he said, "Do not throw what is holy to the dogs, nor toss your pearls in front of pigs" (Matt. 7:6).

The basic idea was this: anyone can figure out literal or historical meaning to a large extent, but only a spiritually oriented believer can discern the spiritual depths that exist within the literal text. In other words, a cognitive comprehension of the Bible is only part of the process of really understanding the Bible. To know nothing but the letter of the

39. I.e., Luke's explanation that the transfiguration was eight days after Jesus's prediction of his death, whereas Mark and Matthew say it was six.
40. Such as God's sanctioned plan for genocide (Num. 33:52).
41. *On First Principles* 4.1.7.
42. *Sermon* 60A.

text (the literal meaning), Origen once argued, is to be like one of the Pharisees or scribes on whom Jesus pronounced "woe" (Matt. 23:13). The reason is that one will construe the Gospel in the same way as the law or as the heretics do because one does not realize that Jesus Christ as the Word is the fulfillment of God's promises.

A literal-only interpretation of the Bible is not an insurance policy against abuse of the Bible's meaning. It might serve as a means for determining a valid explanation in conjunction with other methods, but it should not stand alone. In his sermons on various scriptural passages, the fifth-century pastor Peter Chrysologus claimed, "The historical narrative should always be raised to a higher meaning, and mysteries of the future should become known through figures of the present. Therefore, we should unfold by allegorical discourse what mystical teaching is contained beneath the outward appearance [of the text]."[43] While the literal meaning is an important place for the interpreter to begin, it is perfected by the spiritual understanding that may consist of typological or allegorical or anagogical meanings[44] found within the text. So Augustine exclaims at one point in his *Confessions*:

> What wonderful profundity there is in your utterances! The surface meaning lies open before us and charms beginners. Yet the depth is amazing, my God, the depth is amazing. To focus on its meaning is to experience awe—the awe of adoration before its transcendence and love. (12.14.17)

The patristic approach to the Bible could be haphazard, and sometimes it is difficult to know exactly what the writer was trying to communicate. The early fathers did not share any unifying theory of biblical interpretation. At the same time, we can say that the patristic practice was not allegorizing this or that passage on a whim, but on the basis of a general theological vision. This vision was based foremost on the conviction that Jesus Christ is the fulfillment of the Law and the Prophets, and that the entire Scriptures bear testimony to that fact. It is Christ who brings order and sensibility to the disparate and conflicting data of the Bible. He is the "inner logic" that ties the whole of it together.

Two points immediately emerge from this general vision: the patristic writers perceived themselves as following and continuing the apostolic pattern of exegesis,[45] which meant that they practiced what we might call

43. *Sermon* 36.
44. For definitions of these terms, see chap. 7, below.
45. Cf. Luke 24:44–47. The Law and Prophets proclaimed Christ and his coming, which is perceived only by the "opening of ones' eyes" by faith.

a "total reading" of Scripture.[46] Whereas modern biblical criticism has stressed the unique features behind the history and composition of each of the individual books of the Bible, the ancients were interested in how the Scriptures operated as a unified and interrelated composition, fitting together as a complementary whole.[47] It not only fit together; it also was designed by God so that any one text of Scripture had to be interpreted in light of all the rest of Scripture, both Old and New Testaments. Quite obviously, the notion that Scripture should interpret Scripture was a patristic principle inherited by the sixteenth-century reformers.

Scripture shares an inner coherence and design because of its divine origins, which means that the act of interpretation is in reality a task of unveiling and clarifying the pattern of truths already present in the structure (the very words and sentences). A theology gained from one text can and should inform the construal of other texts. Patristic writers expected to find Pauline perspectives in their reading of the Gospels or Johannine teaching in the Genesis story of creation. Also following the apostolic exegetical pattern, every book of the Bible contributed to a single interpretive scheme: Jesus Christ is the final revelation of God. He is the hermeneutical "key" for unlocking scriptural meaning. It was natural, therefore, for the ancients to find typological, allegorical, and anagogical approaches to the text as necessary for an understanding of the Bible.

The various approaches for discovering the meaning or "senses" inherent to Scripture depend on the formulation of this vision, which then made it possible to discern relationships between God and history, Christ and church, and theology and spirituality. These "senses" varied among ancient writers between three (literal, moral, and mystical or spiritual) or four (literal, moral, anagogical, and allegorical),[48] and even these "senses" could overlap or their definitions vary somewhat from writer to writer. Nevertheless, the basic idea was the same. God had "built" these possible interpretations into the text for the edification and growth of his people. Indeed, the scriptural senses reflected the avenues by which the believer could participate in the life of Christ and "ascend" to God.

Not just any interpretation of a passage was acceptable to the ancients because the rest of Scripture and the tradition served as theological parameters, which effectively limited the possible number of

46. John O'Keefe and Russell Reno, *Sanctified Vision: An Introduction to Early Christian Interpretation of the Bible* (Baltimore: Johns Hopkins University Press, 2005), 25.

47. Peter Gorday, *Principles of Patristic Exegesis: Romans 9–11 in Origen, John Chrysostom, and Augustine* (New York: Mellen, 1983), 36–38.

48. There was no uniform approach in the ancient period; Origen and Jerome follow a tripartite division, whereas a quadripartite delineation is exemplified by Clement of Alexandria, Augustine, and John Cassian. See chaps. 6 and 7, below.

interpretations. There existed, even if spelled out in no one place, a certain hermeneutical "fence" that kept the mystical use of the Bible relatively confined to the conceptual and terminological world of the canonical Scripture.

Again, we recall that the divine nature of the text called for transformation. By this I do not mean merely that reading the Bible changes one's heart. To share in the mystical or allegorical reading of Scripture is to invite the Spirit of God to expand and sharpen the senses of one's heart. As Origen states in his Matthew commentary: "Whenever someone draws near so as to make room for the word, then the kingdom of heaven draws near to such a person."[49] But transformation was also the means by which one was able to perceive God's truth. At this point the ancients took quite literally the beatitude "Blessed are the pure in heart, for they will see God" (Matt. 5:8). Unlike modern emphasis on technique and intellectual skill for effective biblical interpretation, exegesis for the early fathers was a spiritual exercise—itself a sacred task—that demanded the purity and holiness of the interpreter. The use of spiritual or allegorical interpretation was not a hermeneutical "escape hatch," designed to get around the meaning of problematic or conflicting passages without really having to face them. Such passages were regarded as opportunities for God's hand to be seen more clearly. The point of it, in the end, was to draw the believer deeper into the life of God.

Christian Education in the Beginning

A number of texts chosen for this collection are meant to illustrate how seriously the early church took the ministry of training new believers in the faith. This is a point we must not miss. Teaching and learning the Christian faith is time-consuming, demanding of one's commitment, a weighty obligation on church staff, and may create a certain amount of family inconvenience. It was also once a risky affair.[50] Justin "the Martyr" was arrested right in the middle of teaching a group of new Christians in his apartment. All of them were executed. In 202, the renowned female martyr of Carthage, Perpetua, and her fellow believers were arrested and imprisoned. They, too, had been interrupted by soldiers while attend-

49. *Commentary on Matthew* 10.14.
50. As it is in a number of countries today. In China, for example, a number of Christian pastors and small-group leaders have been arrested on trumped-up charges and held in prisons, where they are tortured to "confess" their "crimes." It is striking how this compares with Tertullian's remarks against the Romans' judicial treatment of Christians who had been arrested: "In the case of a robber denying, you apply torture to make them confess—Christians alone you torture to make them deny" (*Apology* 2).

ing a small "class" that was preparing them for baptism. It was said of Perpetua that though she was never baptized in water, she was baptized in her own blood. In Alexandria, Origen led a catechetical "small group" from which came some of the brightest and most deeply committed Christian thinkers of the age.

It is no accident that the earliest development of "Christian education" emerged out of a situation of need. The moments when the early fathers most directly speak of the church's tradition are in apologetic contexts, when they are defending catholic faith against its detractors; and when they are defining the faith, describing it for the needs of catechesis, explaining the faith in the context of instructing new believers for baptism.

There were, of course, no "Sunday school" or regular catechism classes in antiquity. Indeed, we know of no system of Christianizing new Christians before the third century. Slowly but deliberately did the ancient Christian leaders discover that the early formation of a new believer's mind and heart were crucial if they had any hope of the church functioning as a countercultural institution. Yet the education of new converts to Christian thought and practice was no small task. By the middle of the second century, most converts to Christianity were coming out of a classical pagan thought-world, which meant they were religiously syncretistic (having several allegiances to several gods for different reasons) and morally indifferent to (or confused by) the standards expressed in the Beatitudes (unless they came from a philosophical background). Another hurdle for early churches was that most people were functionally illiterate: hence, a large percentage of new Christians had to be taught without the use of texts.

We can learn much from the ancient church's focus on catechesis, on carefully instructing converts or those preparing to join the church in the basic teachings of the Christian faith. In the preface to his manual of Christian instruction, Gregory of Nyssa declared: "Religious catechism is an essential duty of the leaders 'of the mystery of our religion' [1 Tim. 3:16]. By it the church is enlarged through the addition of those who are saved, while 'the sure word which accords with the teaching' [Titus 1:9] comes within the hearing of unbelievers." Gregory would no doubt insist that the teaching of new Christians or new members must go well beyond an initiation into the church's leadership structure and polity of the congregation, issues of stewardship, being acquainted with the "missions" statement, or a brief denominational summary. To introduce the young or a novice to the church of Jesus Christ means opening for them treasures of the central points of the apostolic faith; this faith, larger than any one denomination's or church's claims upon it, is sharpened and transmitted through the ages.

Too often we assume potential church members already know the fundamentals of their faith, whereas in reality they are usually incapable of explaining the basics of "the pattern of sound teaching" (2 Tim. 1:13). This need for equipping cannot be displaced in favor of simply giving one's own testimony any more than to say a personal experience of the faith can be substituted for a reasonable grasp of that faith. If the church, as the apostle phrased it, "is the pillar and foundation of the truth" (1 Tim. 3:15), then ecclesiastical leadership must not shirk from the critical and time-consuming job of imparting Christian truth or catechizing those who profess to be Christian. Nothing can replace the formation of a theologically and biblically literate people. Nothing is more essential for the future vitality of the Christian church.

ORIGINS OF CHRISTIAN TRADITION

A. The Apostle Paul

1. 1 Corinthians 15:1–3

Now, brothers, I want to remind you of the gospel I preached to you, which you received and on which you have taken your stand. By this gospel you are saved, if you hold firmly to the word I preached to you. Otherwise, you have believed in vain. For what I received I passed on to you as of first importance: that Christ died for our sins according to the Scriptures.

2. 1 Corinthians 11:23

I received from the Lord what I also passed on to you: The Lord Jesus, on the night he was betrayed, took bread.

3. 2 Thessalonians 2:15

So then, brothers, stand firm and hold to the teachings we passed on to you, whether by word of mouth or by letter.

By the time Paul wrote his epistles, the church already possessed certain standards of the Christian faith. Using the vibrant language of tradition, Paul says he himself "received" (*paralambanō*) this "gospel" from the Lord, which he also "delivered" (*paradidōmi*) to his readers (1 Cor. 11:23; 15:3). The very word "tradition" is a dynamic term of handing over and receiving, a living and active transmission of the church's preaching. The three verses above represent three modes of the earliest stages of this tradition: doctrinal, liturgical, and ethical. The tradition in 1 Cor. 11 has to do with order of worship, specifically celebrating the Lord's Supper, whereas in 1 Cor. 15, the tradition is about the core of the Christian message. By "traditions" (*paradoseis*) in 2 Thess. 2:15, the emphasis appears to be on ethical tradition, that is, on corporate and personal Christian practices. For a parallel, see Col. 2:6: "Just as you have received (*paralambanō*) Christ Jesus as Lord, continue to live in him."

B. The Apostle Peter

1. Acts 2:22–36: First Preaching of the Christ Tradition

Men of Israel, listen to this: Jesus of Nazareth was a man accredited by God to you by miracles, wonders and signs, which God did among you through him, as you yourselves know. This man was handed over to you by God's set purpose and foreknowledge; and you, with the help of wicked men, put him to death by nailing him to the cross. But God raised him from the dead, freeing him from the agony of death, because it was impossible for death to keep its hold on him. David said about him: "I saw the Lord always before me. Because he is at my right hand, I will not be shaken. Therefore my heart is glad and my tongue rejoices; my body also will live in hope, because you will not abandon me to the grave, nor will you let your Holy One see decay. You have made known to me the paths of life; you will fill me with joy in your presence." Brothers, I can tell you confidently that the patriarch David died and was buried, and his tomb is here to this day. But he was a prophet and knew that God had promised him on oath that he would place one of his descendants on his throne. Seeing what was ahead, he spoke of the resurrection of the Christ, that he was not abandoned to the grave, nor did his body see decay. God has raised this Jesus to life, and we are all witnesses of the fact. Exalted to the right hand of God, he has received from the Father the promised Holy Spirit and has poured out what you now see and hear. For David did not ascend to heaven, and yet he said, "The Lord said to my Lord: 'Sit at my right hand until I make your enemies a footstool for your feet.'" Therefore let all Israel be assured of this: God has made this Jesus, whom you crucified, both Lord and Christ.

2. 1 Peter 3:18–22: The Descent of Christ

For Christ died for sins once for all, the righteous for the unrighteous, to bring you to God. He was put to death in the body, but made alive by the Spirit, through whom also he went and preached to the spirits in prison, who disobeyed long ago when God waited patiently in the days of Noah while the ark was being built. In it only a few people, eight in all, were saved through water, and this water symbolizes baptism that now saves you also. . . . It saves you by the resurrection of Jesus Christ, who has gone into heaven and is at God's right hand—with angels, authorities and powers in submission to him.

A baptismal context is clearly the occasion of these words, and it has been suggested that this passage reads like part paraphrase and part quotation of an instruction preparatory to baptism.[1] The allegorical explanation inserted at verse 20 about the relation of "flood" water to baptismal water seems to vindicate the idea that it is based upon or taken from a catechetical scheme.

C. 1 Clement: Canon of the Tradition (ca. 96)

Therefore let us abandon empty and futile thinking, and conform ourselves to the glorious and holy canon of our tradition. Indeed, let us note what is good and what is pleasing and what is acceptable in the sight of him who made us. (1 Clement 7.2–3; Holmes, Apostolic Fathers, 37)

Written to the Christians in Corinth, the letter known as 1 Clement was probably written from Rome in the closing years of the first century. The writer is unknown, but he is clearly drawing on Paul's letters in support of his own admonishment to the Corinthian Christians that they avoid the church schism among the congregational elders, which is occurring in their midst.

D. Ignatius of Antioch: Christ the Center (ca. 110)

1. To the Ephesians 18.2; 20.2

For our God, Jesus the Christ, was conceived by Mary, in God's plan being sprung both from the seed of David and from the Holy Spirit. He was born and baptized that by his passion he might sanctify water.[2] . . . I have only touched upon this plan in reference to the

1. Kelly, *Early Christian Creeds*, 18.
2. Probable allusion to the believer's baptism in water.

New Man, Jesus Christ, and how it involves believing in him and loving him, and entails his passion and resurrection, . . . and [he] is the Son of Man and the Son of God. (LCC 1:92–93)

2. To the Trallians 9.1–2

Jesus Christ, of David's lineage, of Mary; who was really born, ate, and drank; was really persecuted under Pontius Pilate; was really crucified and died, in the sight of heaven and earth and the underworld [cf. Phil. 2:8–10]. He was really raised from the dead, for his Father raised him [Acts 2:24], just as his Father will raise us who believe on him, through Christ Jesus, apart from whom we have no genuine life. (LCC 1:100)

3. To the Smyrnaeans 1.1–2

Regarding our Lord, you are absolutely convinced that on the human side he was really sprung from David's line [Rom. 1:3], Son of God according to God's will and power, really born of a virgin, baptized by John, so that "all righteousness might be fulfilled by him" [Matt. 3:15], and really crucified for us under Pontius Pilate and Herod the Tetrarch—we are part of the fruit that grew out of his most blessed passion. And thus by his resurrection, he raised a standard [cf. Isa. 5:26; 11:12] to rally his saints and faithful forever, whether Jews or Gentiles, into one body of his church [Eph. 2:16]. (LCC 1:113)

Ignatius's theological emphasis is christological, a point of focus that is frequently utilized throughout his seven authentic letters. Ignatius often points to the reality of Christ's physical passion (sufferings) and resurrection since some Christians, in seeking to preserve the divinity of Christ from the corruption of the flesh, argued that Christ did not live and suffer in the same way that human beings do. It was incumbent upon Ignatius to provide the rudiments of what the faithful were taught about one who was the Son of God and Son of Man. Triadic statements seem also to have been a part of the church's worship and preaching (cf. To the Ephesians 9.1; To the Magnesians 13.1). Again, in many cases, these recitations of the apostolic tradition intentionally functioned to define the boundaries of apostolicity in opposition to erroneous notions.

E. The *Didache*: "Two Ways" Tradition (late 1st–early 2nd cent.)

The teaching of the Lord to the Gentiles by the twelve apostles.
    There are two ways, one of life and one of death, and there is a great difference between these two ways.

Now this is the way of life: first, "you shall love God, who made you"; second, "your neighbor as yourself" [Matt. 22:37–39; Lev. 19:18]; and "whatever you do not wish to happen to you, do not do to another" [cf. Matt. 7:12].

The teaching of these words is this: "Bless those who curse you," and "pray for your enemies," and "fast for those who persecute you." "For what credit is it, if you love those who love you? Do not even the Gentiles do the same?" But "you must love those who hate you" [Matt. 5:44, 46–47; Luke 6:27–28, 32–33], and you will not have an enemy. Abstain from physical and bodily cravings [1 Pet. 2:11]. "If someone gives you a blow on your right cheek, turn to him the other as well," and you will be perfect [Matt. 5:39, 48; Luke 6:29]. If someone "forces you to go one mile, go with him two miles"; "if someone takes your cloak, give him your tunic also" [Matt. 5:41, 40]; "if someone takes from you what belongs to you, do not demand it back," for you cannot do so [Luke 6:30]. "Give to everyone who asks you, and do not demand it back," for the Father wants something from his own gifts to be given to everyone. Blessed is the one who gives according to the command, for such a person is innocent. Woe to the one who receives: if, on the one hand, someone who is in need receives, this person is innocent, but the one who does not have need will have to explain why and for what purpose he received, and upon being imprisoned will be interrogated about what he has done, and will not be released from there until he has repaid every last cent [Matt. 5:26]. But it has also been said concerning this: "Let your gift sweat in your hands until you know to whom to give it."[3]

The second commandment of the teaching is: "You shall not murder; you shall not commit adultery"; you shall not corrupt boys; you shall not be sexually promiscuous; "you shall not steal"; you shall not practice magic; you shall not engage in sorcery; you shall not abort a child or commit infanticide. "You shall not covet your neighbor's possessions; you shall not commit perjury; you shall not give false testimony"; you shall not speak evil; you shall not hold a grudge. You shall not be double-minded, or double-tongued, for the "double-tongue" is a deadly snare [Prov. 21:6]. Your word must not be false or meaningless, but confirmed by action. You shall not be greedy or avaricious, or a hypocrite or malicious or arrogant. You shall not hatch evil plots against your neighbor. You shall not hate anyone; instead you shall reprove some, and pray for some, and some you shall love more than your own life.

---

3. Source unknown. An undocumented saying of Jesus?

My child, flee from evil of every kind, and from every thing resembling it. Do not become angry, for anger leads to murder. Do not be jealous or quarrelsome or hot-tempered, for all these things breed murders. My child, do not be lustful, for lust leads to fornication. Do not be foul-mouthed or let your eyes roam, for all these things breed adultery. My child, do not be an auger,[4] since it leads to idolatry. Do not be an enchanter or an astrologer or a magician, or even desire to see them, for all these things breed idolatry. My child, do not be a liar, since lying leads to theft. Do not be avaricious or conceited, for all these things breed thefts. My child, do not be a grumbler, since it leads to blasphemy. Do not be arrogant or evil-minded, for all these things breed blasphemies.

Instead, be humble, for "the humble shall inherit the earth" [Ps. 37:11; Matt. 5:5]. Be patient and merciful and innocent and quiet and good, and revere always the words which you have heard.[5] Do not exalt yourself or permit your soul to become arrogant. Your soul shall not associate with the lofty, but live with the righteous and the humble. Accept as good the things that happen to you, knowing that nothing transpires apart from God.

My child, night and day remember the one who preaches God's word to you [Heb. 13:7] and honor him as though he were the Lord. For wherever the Lord's nature is preached, there the Lord is. Moreover, you shall seek out daily the presence of the saints, that you may find support in their words. You shall not cause division, but shall make peace between those who quarrel [Deut. 1:16–17, Prov. 31:9]. You shall judge righteously; you shall not show partiality when reproving transgressions. You shall not waver with regard to your decisions.

Do not be someone who stretches out his hands to receive, but withdraws them when it comes to giving. If you earned something by working with your hands, you shall give a ransom for your sins. You shall not hesitate to give, nor shall you grumble when giving, for you shall yet come to know who is the good paymaster of the reward. You shall not turn away from someone in need, but shall share everything with your brother, and not claim that anything is your own [Acts 4:32]. For if you are sharers in what is imperishable, how much more so in perishable things!

You shall not withhold your hand from your son or your daughter, but from their youth you shall teach them the fear of God. You

4. One who attempts to foretell the future by examining the behavior or entrails of birds or animals.
5. Literally, "the teaching," the tradition or instruction received (cf. Isa. 66:2).

shall not give orders to your slave or servant girl (who hope in the same God as you) when you are angry, lest they cease to fear the God who is over you both. For he comes to call not with regard to reputation but upon those whom the Spirit has prepared. And you slaves shall be submissive to your masters in respect and fear, as to a symbol of God.

You shall hate all hypocrisy, and everything that is not pleasing to the Lord. You must not forsake the Lord's commandments, but must guard what you have received, neither adding nor subtracting anything [Deut. 4:2; 12:32]. In church you shall confess your transgressions, and you shall not approach your prayer with an evil conscience. This is the way of life.

But the way of death is this: first of all, it is evil and completely cursed; murders, adulteries, lusts, fornications, thefts, idolatries, magic arts, sorceries, robberies, false testimonies, hypocrisy, duplicity, deceit, arrogance, malice, stubbornness, greed, foul speech, jealousy, audacity, pride, boastfulness. It is the way of persecutors of good people, of those hating truth, loving a lie, not knowing the reward of righteousness, not adhering to what is good or to righteous judgment [Rom. 12:9], being on the alert not for what is good but for what is evil, from whom gentleness and patience are far away, loving worthless things [Ps. 4:2], pursuing profit [Isa. 1:23], having no mercy for the poor, not working on behalf of the oppressed, not knowing him who made them, murderers of children, corrupters of God's creation, turning away from someone in need, oppressing the afflicted, advocates of the wealthy, lawless judges of the poor, utterly sinful. May you be delivered, children, from all these things!

See that no one leads you astray from this way of the teaching, for such a person teaches you without regard for God. For if you are able to bear the whole yoke of the Lord, you will be perfect. But if you are not able, then do what you can. (*Didache* 1.1–6.2; Holmes, *Apostolic Fathers*, 251–57, slightly modified)

One of the earliest catechisms, presenting Christian ethics as the "Two Ways," was circulating in the East by the mid–second century. Three versions of it have come down to us: in the *Epistle of Barnabas* 18–19, in the *Didache*, and in book 7 of the *Apostolic Constitutions*,[6] beginning with

6. The *Epistle of Barnabas* and the *Didache* show close parallels of structure, whereas in the fourth-century *Apostolic Constitutions* the "Two Ways" instruction has been greatly expanded as part of the preparation of candidates for baptism. All three versions show interpolations and glosses on a text that probably originated in Jewish circles. Distinct precedents for the "two ways" ethic are found in Deut. 30:15–20 and the *Manual of Discipline* (1QS) of the Qumran community.

the words, "There are two ways, one of life (or light) and one of death (or darkness); and between the two ways there is a great difference." What follows is a series of ethical injunctions, based on the Sermon on the Mount, directly quoting from Matt. 5 and Luke 6. Jesus's teaching on the lifestyle for the kingdom of God is taken at face value and embraced as authentic Christian living. The catechetical nature of these injunctions is made clear from the fact that they are issued within the context of a congregation: among other things the reader is urged to honor those "who preach God's word to you" (4.1), all forms of schism among believers are condemned (4.3), and the confession of sins in the church assembly before offering prayer is said to be "the way of life" (4.14). That the manual of "Two Ways" was immediately followed by baptismal instructions in the *Didache* and the *Apostolic Constitutions* underscores its original design as a catechism.

F. *2 Clement*: An Early Christian Sermon (early or mid–2nd cent.)

> He has given us the light; as a father, he has called us sons;
> He has saved us when we were perishing.
> What praise shall we give him? What payment in return for
>   what we have received?
>
> Our minds were blinded; we worshipped stones and wood
>   and gold and silver and brass—works of men. Our whole
>   life was nothing else but death.
> We were thus wrapped in darkness and our vision filled
>   with thick mist.
> We recovered our sight by his will, laying aside the cloud
>   which enveloped us.
>
> He had mercy upon us, and in his compassion,
> He saved us when we had no hope of salvation, except
>   what comes from him, and though he had seen in us
>   much deception and destruction.
>
> He called us when we did not exist, and out of nothing,
> He willed us into being.
>
> (*2 Clement* 1.4–8; a lyrical rendering of Holmes,
>   *Apostolic Fathers*, 107)

The above has some confessional or liturgical qualities that appear in the beginning of the sermon, hence it has been presented in verse fashion. Having no relation whatsoever to the text known as *1 Clement*, the anonymous *2 Clement* has all the characteristics of a sermon, delivered in the context of an early second-century Jewish Christian community.

G. Polycarp of Smyrna: The Gospel of Christ (ca. 155)

"Therefore prepare for action and serve God in fear" [1 Pet. 1:13; cf. Ps. 2:11] and truth, leaving behind the empty and meaningless talk and the error of the crowd, and "believing in him who raised" our Lord Jesus Christ "from the dead and gave him glory" [1 Pet. 1:21] and a throne at his right hand; to whom all things in heaven and on earth were subjected [cf. 1 Cor. 15:28; Phil. 2:10; 3:21], whom every breathing creature serves, who is coming as "Judge of the living and the dead" [Acts 10:42], for whose blood God will hold responsible those who disobey him [cf. Luke 11:50–51]. But "he who raised him from the dead will raise us also" [cf. 2 Cor. 4:14]; if we do his will and follow in his commandments and love the things he loved, while avoiding every kind of unrighteousness, greed, love of money, slander, and false testimony; "not repaying evil for evil or insult for insult" [1 Pet. 3:9] or blow for blow or curse for curse, but instead remembering what the Lord said as he taught: "Do not judge, that you may not be judged; forgive, and you will be forgiven; show mercy, that you may be shown mercy: with the measure you use, it will be measured back to you" [Matt. 7:1–2; cf. Luke 6:36–38]; and "blessed are the poor and those who are persecuted for righteousness' sake, for theirs is the kingdom of God" [Luke 6:20; Matt. 5:10; cf. Matt. 5:3]. (*Epistle to the Philippians* 2.1–3; *Creeds and Confessions*, 44)

Polycarp was bishop of Smyrna (now Izmir on the west coast of Turkey) from the beginning of the second century until his death around AD 156. According to Irenaeus, Polycarp had actually met the disciple John and others who had seen Jesus Christ while he lived on earth. This connection to the apostolic age and his own martyrdom made Polycarp an authoritative voice in early Christianity. In the account of his martyrdom, he is referred to as "an apostolic and prophetic teacher and bishop" (16.2).

H. Justin the Martyr: Explaining the Christian Faith (ca. 155)

After these [services] we constantly remind each other of these things. Those who have more come to the aid of those who lack, and we are constantly together. Over all that we receive we bless the Maker of all things through his Son Jesus Christ and through the Holy Spirit. And on the day called Sunday there is a meeting in one place of those who live in cities or the country, and the memoirs of the apostles or the writings of the prophets are read as long as time permits. When the reader has finished, the president in a discourse urges and invites [us] to the imitations of these noble things. Then we all stand up together and offer prayers. And, as said before, when we have finished the prayer, bread is brought, and wine and water, and the president similarly sends up prayers and thanksgivings to the best of his ability, and the congregation assents, saying the Amen; the distribution, and reception of the consecrated [elements] by each one, takes place and they are sent to the absent by the deacons. Those who prosper and who so wish, contribute each one as much as he chooses to. What is collected is deposited with the president,[7] and he takes care of orphans and widows, and those who are in want on account of sickness or any other cause, and those who are in bonds, and the strangers who are sojourners among [us], and, briefly, he is the protector of all those in need. We all hold this common gathering on Sunday, since it is the first day, on which God transforming darkness and matter made the universe, and Jesus Christ our Savior rose from the dead on the same day. For they crucified him on the day before Saturday, and on the day after Saturday, he appeared to his apostles and disciples and taught them these things which I have passed on to you also for your serious consideration. (*1 Apology* 67; LCC 1:287–88)

Justin of Rome (also known as Justin the Martyr) was converted to Christianity in his early adulthood, having sought for the truth among various philosophical schools such as the Stoics, Aristotelians, and the Platonists. He set up a "school" for Christian philosophy in Rome, which was likely a catechetical group for the church of Rome. His *Apology*, one of several works attributed to him, was modeled on Plato's *Apologia*: a defense of those wrongly accused. It was published during the reign of the emperor Antoninus Pious (AD 138–61) and represents the first major intellectual description of Christian belief and practice that survives. Around the year 165, Justin was arrested along with some pupils and executed for his Christian confession.

I. Anonymous Homily concerning the Mystery of Faith (mid or late 2nd cent.)

The things that pertain to the tradition I try to minister appropriately to those who are becoming disciples of the truth. Can anyone who has been properly taught and has come to love the Logos, keep from trying to learn precisely what has been shown openly by the Logos to those to whom he openly appeared and spoke in the

7. That is, the one who presides over that believing community.

plainest terms? He remained, indeed, unrecognized by unbelievers, but he gave a full explanation to his disciples who, because he looked upon them as faithful, came to know the mysteries of the Father.

For this reason the Father sent the Logos[8] to appear in the world—the Logos who was slighted by the chosen people, but preached by apostles and believed in by the Gentiles. This is he who was from the beginning, who appeared new and was found to be old, and is ever born young in the hearts of the saints.

This is the eternal one, who today is accounted a Son, by whom the church is made rich and grace is multiplied as it unfolds among the saints—the grace that gives understanding, makes mysteries plain, announces seasons, rejoices in believers, is given freely to seekers, that is, to those who do not break the pledges of their faith, or go beyond the bounds set by the fathers. Then the reverence taught by the Law is hymned, and the grace given to the Prophets is recognized, and the faith of the Gospels is made secure, and the tradition of the apostles is maintained, and the grace of the church exults. (Text II of the *Letter to Diognetus*; LCC 1:222–23, slightly adapted)

Although the text above is attached to a letter addressed to Diognetus, implying the two were a unity, it is clear that it is a separate homily appended to the letter, probably written by a different author. It nevertheless offers an authentic portrait of Christianity emerging in the second century as it sought to articulate a doctrine of Christ as discovered both in the Law and Prophets, and the Gospels and the Apostles (letters). A significant tension within the early tradition was how the words and deeds of Christ and their interpretation by the apostles correlated to the Hebrew Bible, or Old Testament.

J. Irenaeus of Lyons: The Single Household of the Faith (ca. 178)

The church, having received this preaching and this faith, although scattered throughout the whole world, yet, as if occupying but one house, carefully preserves it. She[9] also believes these points [of doctrine] just as if she had but one soul, and one and the same heart, and she proclaims them, and teaches them, and hands them

---

8. The Logos, being the Greek term for "word," "mind," "intellect," was associated with the preincarnate Christ. This is the term used in the prologue of John's Gospel: "In the beginning was the Word, and the Word was with God, and the Word was God. . . . And the Word was made flesh and dwelt among us" (1:1, 14).

9. "She" refers here to "the church," a feminine noun in Greek.

down, with perfect harmony, as if she possessed only one voice [Acts 4:32]. For, although the languages of the world are dissimilar, yet the power of the tradition is one and the same. For the churches which have been planted in Germany do not believe or hand down anything different, nor do those in Spain, nor those in Gaul, nor those in the East, nor those in Egypt, nor those in Libya, nor those that have been established in the central regions of the world. But as the sun, a creature of God, is one and the same throughout the whole world, so also the preaching of the truth shines everywhere, and illuminates all men who are willing to come to a knowledge of the truth. Nor will any one of the rulers in the churches, however highly gifted he may be in point of eloquence, teach doctrines different from these (for no one is greater than the Master) [Matt. 10:24]; nor, on the other hand, will someone who is weak in power of expression bring damage on the tradition. For the faith being ever one and the same, neither does one who is able to talk about it at great length, make any addition to it, nor does one, who can say but little diminish it. (*Against Heresies* 1.10.2; *ANF* 1:331; cf. *Irenaeus of Lyons*, ed. Robert M. Grant [London: Routledge, 1997], 71, slightly modified)

As a pastor, Irenaeus's chief concern here is not defending the tradition as much as it is showing that the tradition, like a glue, serves to keep the church unified wherever it is found in the world. Admittedly, churches in different regions have different characteristics and practice. But they share a common tradition that provides a theological centricity in the transmission and proclamation of the church's faith. As the church grows and becomes more varied, the basis of its existence will remain preserved in the earlier churches.

K. Hippolytus of Rome: *Apostolic Tradition* (ca. 215)

Prologue[10]

We have set forth as was necessary that part of the discourse which relates to the spiritual gifts, all that God, right from the beginning, granted to people according to his will, bringing back to himself this image (of God), which had gone astray.

Now, driven by love toward all the saints, we turn to the essence of the tradition which is proper for the churches. This is so that those who are well instructed may hold fast to the tradition that has continued until now, and fully understanding it they may stand

10. This work is fragmented, and it is apparent that some instructions on spiritual gifts (now missing) had already been given.

the more firmly (against the fall or error which has recently occurred because of ignorance and ignorant people). The Holy Spirit
bestows the fullness of grace on those who believe rightly, so that
they will know that those who are at the head of the church must
teach and guard all these things.

Congregational Liturgy and Prayer

The Lord be with you.
And all reply:
And with your spirit.
The bishop says:
Raise your hearts.
The people respond:
We have them with the Lord.
The bishop says:
Let us give thanks to the Lord.
The people respond:
It is proper and just.
The bishop then continues:
We give thanks to you, God,
through your beloved son Jesus Christ,
whom you sent to us in former times[11]
as Savior, Redeemer, and Messenger of your will,
who is your inseparable Word,
through whom you made all things,
and in whom you were well-pleased,
whom you sent from heaven into the womb of a virgin,
who, being conceived within her, was made flesh,
and appeared as your Son,
born of the Holy Spirit and the Virgin.
It is he who, fulfilling your will
and acquiring for you a holy people,
extended his hands in suffering,
in order to liberate from sufferings
those who believe in you.
Who, when he was delivered to voluntary suffering,
in order to dissolve death,
and break the chains of the devil,
and tread down hell,
and bring the just to the light,

11. Or "in the last days."

and set the limit,
and manifest the resurrection.
. . . .
And we pray that you would send your Holy Spirit
to the oblation of your holy church.
In their gathering together,
give to all those who partake of your holy mysteries the
    fullness of the Holy Spirit,
toward the strengthening of the faith in truth,
that we may praise you and glorify you,
through your son Jesus Christ,
through whom to you be glory and honor,
Father and Son,
with the Holy Spirit,
in your holy church,
now and throughout the ages of the ages.
Amen.

(based on Gregory Dix, *The Treatise on the Apostolic
Tradition of St. Hippolytus of Rome, Bishop and Martyr*
[London: SPCK, 1937], 7–9)

This prayer is part (section 4) of a longer set of instructions intended for church leaders conducting the life and piety of the church of Rome. The *Apostolic Tradition* (title is taken from the epilogue) is attributed to the Roman presbyter Hippolytus, though the authorship is not certain. Numerous subjects are briefly touched upon that have to do with the life of the church body (procedures for ordaining clergy and the appropriate prayers, the process of teaching catechumens, the steps of baptism, etc.), which makes this text appear to be a manual to regulate church practice.

THE INTERPLAY
OF SCRIPTURE
AND TRADITION

A. Ignatius of Antioch: Scripture and Gospel Tradition (ca. 110)

When I heard some people saying, "If I don't find it in the original documents,[1] I don't believe it in the gospel." I answered them, "But it is written there." They retorted, "That's just the question." To my mind it is Jesus Christ who is the original documents. The inviolable archives are his cross and death and his resurrection and the faith that came by him. (*To the Philadelphians* 8.2; LCC 1:110)

There was no doubt among the earliest Christians that there existed a prophetic and historical continuity between the Old Testament and the apostolic preaching. Exactly what sort of continuities could or should be claimed was a matter of debate. Nevertheless, it was therefore expected that one could find any central truth pertaining to the Christian faith in the pages of the Old Testament provided that one used the "lens" of the gospel or apostolic tradition to read it.

1. The Old Testament.

B. Justin the Martyr: When the Hebrew Prophets Are Rightly Read (ca. 165)

There existed long before our time certain men who were more ancient than all those who are esteemed philosophers.[2] These were esteemed both righteous and beloved by God, and they spoke by the divine Spirit, and foretold events which would take place, and which are now taking place. They are called prophets. These alone both saw and announced the truth to humanity, neither reverencing nor fearing any man, not influenced by a desire for glory, but speaking those things alone which they saw and which they heard, being filled with the Holy Spirit.

Their writings still survive, and whoever reads them is greatly helped in his knowledge of the beginning and end of things, and of those matters that the philosopher ought to know[3]—provided he has believed them. For they did not use physical proofs in their treatises, seeing that they were themselves witnesses to the truth, which was better than having proofs. The things they wrote are worthy of belief, and those very events which have happened and which are now happening should convince you to accept the utterances made by them.

At the same time, however, the prophets were entitled to recognition on account of the miracles that they performed, since they both glorified the Creator, the God and Father of all things, and proclaimed his Son, the Christ sent by him. So pray that, above all things, the gates of light may be opened to you; for these things[4] cannot be perceived or understood by just anyone, but only by the person to whom God and his Christ have imparted wisdom. (*Dialogue with Trypho* 7; ANF 1:198, significantly modified)

In his reputed debate with Trypho, an intellectual Jew, Justin wants to show how the Hebrew Scriptures are to be properly interpreted so that they reveal the birth, ministry, death and resurrection of Christ. For Justin, the ancient prophets were the means of God's revelation, superior to any philosophical wisdom. But he also implicitly supported and taught that the church's tradition was the means of interpreting the Jewish Bible. Part of Justin's rationale

---

2. Elsewhere Justin argues, not uncommonly, that the ancient prophets of the Old Testament, such as Abraham and Moses, lived before Socrates and Plato.

3. Because the prophets preceded the Greek philosophers, it was believed that the latter had taken some of the prophetic truths into their own philosophical systems. For this reason, some truth could be found in writers such as Plato, though reading the ancient Hebrew prophets was superior to any philosopher.

4. The words and acts of the ancient prophets.

was that God's Logos (or Word)[5] was one who had appeared and inspired the Old Testament authors, and in the last days, this Word became incarnate as Jesus Christ. It follows, therefore, that the prophets would speak about Christ, the living Word of God.

C. Irenaeus of Lyons (ca. 178)

1. Apostolic Writings and Tradition

We have learned from no others the plan of our salvation, than from those through whom the gospel has come down to us, which they once proclaimed in public, and, by the will of God at a later point, handed down to us in the Scriptures, to be the ground and pillar of our faith (1 Tim. 3:15). For it is unlawful to assert that they preached before they possessed "perfect knowledge," as some do even venture to say,[6] boasting themselves as improvers of the apostles. For the apostles, after our Lord rose from the dead, were imbued with power from on high when the Holy Spirit came down upon them, were filled with all his gifts, and had perfect knowledge. They departed to the ends of the earth, preaching the glad tidings of the good things sent from God to us, and proclaiming the peace of heaven to men, who indeed do all equally and individually possess the gospel of God.

Matthew also issued a written Gospel among the Hebrews in their own dialect, while Peter and Paul were preaching at Rome, laying the foundations of the church. After their departure, Mark, the disciple and interpreter of Peter, did also hand down to us in writing what had been preached by Peter. Luke also, the companion of Paul, recorded in a book the gospel preached by him. Afterward, John, the disciple of the Lord, who also had leaned upon his breast, did himself publish a Gospel during his residence at Ephesus in Asia.

These have all declared to us that there is one God, Creator of heaven and earth, announced by the Law and the Prophets; and one Christ the Son of God. If any one does not agree to these truths, he despises the companions of the Lord. Moreover, he despises Christ the Lord himself, and even despises the Father also. Such

---

5. "The Word of Wisdom, who is Himself this God begotten of the Father of all things, ... proves my position as he speaks by Solomon the following [quotes Prov. 8:21–28]" (*Dialogue with Trypho* 61 [*ANF* 1:227]).

6. Viz., the gnostic Christians, who declared that God's revelation was not complete or "perfect" without recourse to special writings of lesser known apostles (e.g., *Gospel of Thomas*).

a person stands self-condemned, resisting and opposing his own salvation, as is the case with all heretics.

But, again, when we refer them[7] to that tradition which originates from the apostles, and which is preserved by means of the succession of presbyters in the churches, they object to tradition, saying that they themselves are wiser not merely than the presbyters, but even than the apostles, because they have discovered the unadulterated truth. . . . It comes to this, therefore, that these men do now consent neither to Scripture nor to tradition. (*Against Heresies* 3.1.1–2; 3.2.2; *ANF* 1:414–15, slightly modified)

The reality of the church's faith necessarily entailed a physical presence that could be identified. Apostolicity is thus spelled out as the church's ability to trace its theological and historical lineage back to the apostles. As the two examples from the churches of Rome and Asia Minor show, the concept of succession of churches and their pastors had a quite tangible quality for Irenaeus. A "spiritual-only" interpretation of succession (gnostic) was advocated by his adversaries, who stressed the spiritual transmission of truth for any enlightened Christian. The chief implication is that the church (where exists the confluence of Scripture, tradition, and founding elders) is the only context by which the true faith can be properly expounded because the church is the original recipient of that faith.

2. A Hypothetical Situation to Make a Point

Suppose a dispute concerning some important question arose among us; should we not have recourse to the most ancient churches with which the apostles held constant communion,[8] and learn from them (the churches) what is certain and clear in regard to the present question? For how should it be if the apostles themselves had not left us writings? Would it not be necessary, in that case, to follow the course of the tradition which they handed down to those to whom they did commit the churches?

It is with this tradition that many nations of those barbarians who believe in Christ agree, having salvation written in their hearts by the Spirit, without paper or ink, and carefully preserving the ancient tradition [2 Thess. 2:15; 3:6], believing in one God, the Creator of heaven and earth, and all things therein, by means of Christ Jesus, the Son of God; who, because of his surpassing love toward his creation, condescended to be born of the Virgin, he himself uniting man through himself to God, and having suffered under Pontius Pilate, and rising again, and having been received

7. The Gnostics.
8. Irenaeus has the churches of Ephesus, Smyrna, and Rome in mind.

up in splendor, shall come in glory, the Savior of those who are saved, and the Judge of those who are judged, and sending into eternal fire those who transform the truth, and despise his Father and his advent.

There are those who, in the absence of written documents, have believed this faith. These are barbarians insofar as it concerns our language, but as regards to doctrine, manner, and tenor of life, they are, because of faith, very wise. They please God, ordering their conversation in all righteousness, chastity, and wisdom. If any one were to preach to these people the novelties of the heretics, speaking to them in their own language, they would at once stop their ears, and flee as far off as possible, not enduring even to listen to the blasphemous address. Thus, by means of that ancient tradition of the apostles, they do not allow their minds to conceive anything of the doctrines suggested by the portentous language of these erroneous teachers, among whom neither church nor doctrine has ever been established. (*Against Heresies* 3.4.1–2; *ANF* 1:416–17, slightly modified)

Irenaeus's appeal to the sufficiency of tradition alone was a polemical tactic he used when pushed to the extreme. The Gnostic claimed the same Scriptures as the catholics (sometimes adding other books), yet they constructed a very different view of Christ and God's plan of salvation. Of necessity, the ideal structure of authority for Irenaeus was multilevel: Scripture, tradition, and the church. Like a three-legged stool, these elements acted as the foundation for determining orthodox doctrine. Such an arrangement acted like spiritual checks and balances, which guided the church in its decision-making and served to protect the church from seductive voices that offered new or special revelation, or an alien interpretation of Scripture. Whatever claims to authority that a Christian leader might make, they must be channeled through this trifocal lens of the apostolic faith.

D. Tertullian of Carthage

1. Abuse of Scripture by the Gnostics (ca. 200)

What sort of truth is that which they patronize, when they commend it to us with a lie? Well, they actually treat the Scriptures and recommend their opinions out of the Scriptures! Of course they do. From what other source could they derive their arguments concerning the things of the faith except from the records of the faith?

Now this heresy of theirs does not accept certain Scriptures; but whichever of them it does accept, it perverts by means of additions and deletions for their own purposes. The Scriptures that they do accept, they do so not in their entirety. But when they accept them up to a certain point as entire, they still pervert even these by contriving different interpretations. Truth is just as much opposed by an adulteration of its meaning as it is by a corruption of its text.[9] Their own empty assumptions actually reject an acknowledgement of the (writings) by which they are refuted. They rely on those writings which they have falsely put together, and which they have selected, because of their ambiguity. Though certainly skilled in the Scriptures, they will make no progress, when everything which they claim is denied on the other side, and whatever they deny is (by us) maintained. As for them, in fact, they will lose nothing but their breath, and gain nothing but blasphemy for their efforts. (*On the Prescription of Heretics* 14.17; ANF 3:250–51, modified)

Tertullian is not trying to subordinate the authority of Scripture to tradition. Scripture is fully sufficient for declaring God's truth, and whatever it teaches is unconditionally true. But he argues that the exigencies of doctrinal heresy make it necessary to emphasize one over the other in order to defend the integrity of both. There is actually an inviolable unity between the two such that to reject tradition is to reject Scripture and vice versa. One cannot use the Scriptures and refuse to submit to the teaching of the tradition. Likewise, one cannot claim the tradition in support of a teaching that is denied or not supported in Scripture.

2. "Who Are the Rightful Owners of Scripture?" (ca. 200)

They put forward the Scriptures, and by this act of daring they influence some immediately. In the encounter with others, however, they weary the strong [with their arguments], snare the weak, and confuse those who are hesitant with doubts. Accordingly, we oppose them in this process beyond all others by not admitting them to any kind of discussion of the Scriptures.

If their resources lie in the Scriptures, we ought to discover, before they can use them, to whom belongs the possession of the Scriptures, so that no one may be admitted to their use who has no title at all to the privilege.

We must not appeal to Scripture, nor must a debate be allowed on points in which victory will either be impossible, or uncertain, or not certain enough. . . . The only point that we should discuss is, who holds the faith to which the Bible belongs, and from whom, through whom, when and to whom was the teach-

---

9. Those who claim that the whole message of Christ was left out by certain Scriptures, or that the biblical texts have been tampered with.

ing delivered by which men became Christians? For only where
the true Christian teaching and faith are evident, will be the true
Scriptures, the true interpretations, and all the true Christian
traditions be found. (*On the Prescription of Heretics* 15.19; *ANF*
3:250–51, altered)

Because scriptural interpretation was so often at issue between catholics (mainline Christians) and various forms of Gnosticism, it became clear to Tertullian that any appeal to the Bible
alone was impossible. Tertullian therefore addresses himself to the problem of authority once
he recognized that heresies also used scriptural support for their positions.

He was casting no aspersion on the central importance of Scripture here, but when it became
the point of contention, a point of order had to be made. Tertullian therefore draws our attention to the preliminary issue that must first be answered. It is necessary to show what ground
of authority can be adduced that would entitle one to the access of Scripture. This prior point
of order (*praescriptio*) must be proved before one can claim biblical authority.

3. Tradition Handed On by the Churches (ca. 200)

After Judas had been removed, he [Jesus] commanded the eleven
others, as he was departing to the Father, to "go and teach *all* nations, who were to be baptized into the Father, and into the Son,
and into the Holy Ghost" [Matt. 28:19]. Immediately, therefore, so
did the apostles, whom this designation ("apostles") indicates as
"*the sent.*" On the authority of a prophecy that occurs in a psalm
of David, they chose Matthias by lot as the twelfth, into the place
of Judas, and they obtained the promised power of the Holy Ghost
for the gift of miracles and of utterance. After first bearing witness
to the faith in Jesus Christ throughout Judea and the surrounding
churches, they next went forth into the world and preached the
same doctrine of the same faith to the nations.

Likewise, they then founded churches in every city, from which
all the other churches, one after another, received the tradition
of the faith and the seeds of doctrine, and every day continue to
receive them, so that they may become churches. Indeed, it is for
this reason only that they are able to consider themselves apostolic,
being the offspring of apostolic churches.

Therefore the churches, although they are so many and so great,
comprise but the one primitive church, founded by the apostles,
from which they all spring. In this way all are primitive and all are
apostolic, while they are all proved to be one, in (unbroken) unity,
by their peaceful communion, and title of brotherhood, and bond

of hospitality, and privileges, which no other rule directs than the one tradition of the selfsame mystery.[10] . . .

Since this is the case, in order that the truth may be judged to belong to us, "as many as walk according to the rule," which the church has handed down from the apostles, the apostles from Christ, *and* Christ from God, the reason of our position is clear: it determines that heretics ought not be allowed to challenge from appeal to the Scriptures, since we, without the Scriptures,[11] can prove that they have nothing to do with the Scriptures. For as they are heretics, they cannot be true Christians, because it is not from Christ that they get that which they pursue of their own mere choice, and from the pursuit incur and admit the name of heretics. Thus, not being Christians, they have received no right to the Christian Scriptures. (*On the Prescription of Heretics* 20; *ANF* 3:252, modifed)

4. Antiquity and Truth of Written Revelation (ca. 197)

So that we might obtain a fuller and more authoritative knowledge at once of himself and of his counsels and will, God has added a written revelation for the benefit of everyone whose heart is set on seeking him; that seeking he may find, and finding believe, and believing obey. For from the first he sent messengers into the world—men whose stainless righteousness made them worthy to know the Most High, and to reveal him—men abundantly endowed with the Holy Spirit, that they might proclaim that there is only one God who made all things, who formed man from the dust of the ground.

Their great antiquity [the Scriptures], first of all, provides authority for these writings.[12] With you, too[13], it is a kind of religion to demand belief on this very ground. Well, all the substances, all the materials, the origins, classes, contents of your most ancient writings, . . . your very gods themselves, your very temples and oracles, and sacred rites, are less ancient than the work of a single prophet, in whom you have the *thesaurus* of the entire Jewish religion, and therefore of ours also.[14]

10. "Mystery" here refers to the Christian faith or rule.

11. In other words, the Rule (or tradition) of Faith so closely mirrors the teaching of Scripture that the tradition itself can guide orthodox Christians into truth without the Scriptures.

12. The Hebrew Bible, or as Christians came to call it, the Old Testament.

13. Roman pagans.

14. Tertullian is following a precedent already established in Christian self-understanding, taking the Old Testament as a prophetic declaration of Christ and the gospel as well

Of even greater importance, we may point to the majesty of our Scriptures, if not to their antiquity. If you doubt that they are as ancient as we say, we offer proof that they are divine. And you may convince yourselves of this right away and without going very far. Your instructors, the world, and the age, and their events are all in front of you. All that is taking place around you . . . was all foreseen and predicted before it came to pass. As we suffer the calamities, we read of them in the Scriptures; as we examine, they are proved. Well, the truth of a prophecy, I think, is the demonstration of its being from above. Hence, there is among us an assured faith in regard to coming events as things already proved to us, for they were predicted along with what we have day by day fulfilled. They are uttered by the same voices, they are written in the same books—the same Spirit inspires them. (*Apology* 18–20; *ANF* 3:32–33, altered)

Among the earliest of Tertullian's works, his *Apology* was addressed to a pagan audience, providing an aggressive defense of the Christian position. One of the accusations against the validity of the Christian message was its relative novelty compared to the antiquity of pagan poets and philosophers. The rule for acceptable religion in the Greco-Roman world is invoked by the pagan Caelius in Minucius Felix's *Octavius* (ca. AD 200): "As a general principle, the greater the age that ceremonies and shrines accumulate, the more hallowed these institutions become." In an age that prized antiquity as the key criterion for intellectual reliability and social propriety, the Jewish linking of its identity to ancient traditions often helped to mitigate, though by no means erase, Roman suspicion.

E. Origen: Inspiration and Interpretation of the Scriptures (ca. 250)

We shall now outline the manner in which divine Scripture should be understood on these several points, using such illustrations and examples as may occur to us. And in the first place we must call to mind and point out that the Holy Spirit, who by the providence and will of God through the power of his only-begotten Word, who was "in the beginning with God" [John 1:1], enlightened the servants of the truth, that is, the prophets and apostles. . . .

These mysteries which were made known and revealed to them by the Spirit, the prophets portrayed figuratively through the narration of what seemed to be human deeds and the handing down

---

as related future events. This meant, in effect, that the Hebrew Bible was no less a part of the Christian Scripture.

of certain legal ordinances and precepts.[15] The aim was that not everyone who wished should have these mysteries laid before his feet to trample upon, but that they should be for the one who had devoted himself to studies of this kind with the utmost purity and sobriety and through nights of watching,[16] by which means he might be able to trace out the deeply hidden meaning of the Spirit of God, concealed under the language of an ordinary narrative which points in a different direction, and that so he might become a sharer of the Spirit's knowledge and a partaker of his divine counsel.[17]

For in no other way can the soul reach the perfection of knowledge except by being inspired with the truth of the divine wisdom. Therefore it is chiefly the doctrine about God, that is, about the Father, Son, and Holy Spirit, which is indicated by those [prophets and apostles] who were filled with the divine Spirit. So too, the mysteries relating to the Son of God, how the Word became flesh, and for what reason he went to the length of "taking upon him the form of a servant" [Phil. 2:7], have also been made known by those who were filled, as we have said, with the divine Spirit. (*On First Principles* 4.2, 7; Butterworth, *Origen*, 282–83)

In his preface to this work, Origen made it clear that there existed a "rule" by which our understanding of Scripture is aided and guided. So when Origen talked about the "deeply hidden meaning of the Spirit of God," his intention was not like the Gnostics, who also sought deep and mysterious truths unavailable to the unenlightened. Rather, we should see the "doctrine about God" is found by the discerning believer in the Scripture by means of the Spirit of God.

F. Cyril of Jerusalem: To Those Preparing for Baptism (ca. 350)

Now the one and only faith that you are to take and preserve in the way of learning and professing is being committed to you by the church as confirmed throughout the Scriptures. For seeing that not everyone can read the Scriptures, some because they lack the learning,[18] and others because, for one reason or another, they find no opportunity to get to know them, we can acquire the whole doctrine of the Christian faith in a few articles and so prevent any soul from being lost by not learning the faith.

15. The Mosaic law.
16. That is, prayer.
17. In other words, that the spiritually discerning reader may see in the Law and narratives the deeper meanings that God intended to be found therein.
18. They are illiterate.

At this stage listen to the exact form of words[19] and memorize this faith, leaving it to the appropriate time when each article it contains may be built up from Holy Scripture. For these articles of our faith were not composed out of human opinion, but are the principal points collected out of the whole of Scripture to complete a single doctrinal formulation of the faith. And just as the mustard seed contains many future tree branches within its tiny grain, so also this faith[20] embraces in a few phrases all the religious knowledge contained in the Old and New Testaments together. Be sure, brothers, to "hold the traditions" [2 Thess. 2:15] which are being imparted to you, and "write them on the table of your hearts" [Prov. 7:3]. (*Catechetical Lectures* 5.12; LCC 4:123–24)

Each article of the Jerusalem Creed, as Cyril the bishop expounds them, is so thoroughly grounded in biblical authority that, as the bishop insists, his hearers must not accept anything without reference to the sacred Scriptures. "Do not simply take my word when I tell you these things, unless you are given proof for my teaching from Holy Scripture." Cyril's intention was to assure the catechumens that nothing in the Jerusalem Creed was contrary to the biblical message. Being schooled in the creed was the first step in learning not only what the Bible meant but also in preparing these candidates to read the Bible with insight. The task of presenting the church's faith to new converts usually fell to the bishop.

G. Ambrose of Milan: The Symbol of the Apostles' Teaching (ca. 390)

Now I have often put you in mind that our Lord Jesus Christ, the Son of God, alone took to himself this flesh of ours, together with a human soul rational and perfect. And he took to himself a bodily form: in the reality of this our body he was made as man [Phil. 2:7]. But he has the singular privilege of (the manner of) his generation. For he was not born of the seed of man, but generated, it says, by the Holy Spirit of Mary the virgin. You recognize the prerogative of the heavenly Author: he was made indeed as man, that he might take to himself our infirmities in his own flesh, but he came with the privilege of eternal majesty. So then let us say the Symbol. And when he had said it he went on thus: this is what the divine Scripture has: ought we with reckless mind to go beyond the limits of the Apostles' teaching? Are we more

19. A reference to the (Jerusalem) creed (see chap. 5.A.2, below), which these catechumens are learning.
20. Here "faith" implies the creed.

careful than the Apostles? (*Explanation of the Symbol* 5; Connolly, *Explanatio*, 20–21)

Like Rufinus of Aquileia and others of his era, Ambrose accepted the view that each of the twelve apostles was responsible for writing a portion of the church's creed or "Symbol." Thus, the church's Symbol has been handed down to the churches since apostolic times, which is why the creed is truly apostolic. But Ambrose goes on to say that the Symbol is apostolic because it is an epitome of what the Bible teaches. To go beyond the church's faith as expressed in the Symbol is to ignore the apostles' teaching.

H. Augustine: Setting Out the Catholic Faith for Interpreting Scripture (ca. 393–94)

Before we undertake the study of this book of Genesis, we must briefly set out the catholic faith.

Here then it is: that God the almighty Father made and established the whole of creation through his only-begotten Son, that is, through his wisdom and power consubstantial and co-eternal with himself, in the unity of the Holy Spirit, who is also consubstantial and co-eternal. So Catholic teaching bids us believe that this Trinity is called one God, and that he made and created all things that are, insofar as they are, to the effect that all creatures, whether intellectual or corporeal, or what more briefly according to the words of the divine Scriptures can be called invisible or visible, are not born of God, but made by God out of nothing, and that there is nothing among them which belongs to the Trinity, except what the Trinity created—this nature was created. For this reason it is not lawful to say or believe that the whole creation is consubstantial or co-eternal with God.

Again, that all things that God made, however, are very good [Gen. 1:31], while evil things are not part of nature, but everything that is called evil is either sin or the punishment of sin, and sin is nothing but the twisted consent of the free will, when we stoop to things forbidden by justice which it is true freedom to abstain from. That is, sin consists not in the things themselves, but in the unlawful use of them. Now the use of things is lawful when the soul remains within the bounds of God's law and subject to the one God in unqualified love, and regulates other things that are subject to it without greed or lust, that is, in accordance with God's commandments. It is in this way, you see, that it will exercise control over them without any trouble or distress, and with the greatest ease and felicity.

The punishment though of sin is when the soul is tormented by created things themselves not being at its service, seeing that it declines to be itself at the service of God; this creation was once upon a time compliant to the soul, when the soul was compliant to God. And so there is nothing evil about fire, since it is a creature of God; but all the same we in our frailty get burned by it as our sins justly deserve.

Again, that there are sins, however, which are said to be natural, because we cannot help committing them before God's mercy comes to the rescue, after we have fallen into this condition of life through the sin committed by free will.

Again, that humanity was made new once more through our Lord Jesus Christ, when God's inexpressible and unchangeable Wisdom herself deigned to take on full and complete humanity and to be born of the Holy Spirit and the virgin Mary, to be crucified, to be buried and rise again and ascend into heaven, which has all happened already; and to come to judge the living and the dead at the end of the age and the resurrection of the dead in the flesh, which is proclaimed as being yet to come; that the Holy Spirit has been given to those who believe in him, that mother Church has been established by him, which is called catholic insofar as it has been in all respects perfected and is in no way defective and has spread through the whole wide world; that their previous sins have been forgiven to those who are repentant; and in eternal life and the promise of the kingdom of heaven. (*Unfinished Literal Commentary on Genesis* 1.1–4; WSA 1/13:114–15)

In this second of three commentaries published on Genesis, Augustine first sets about establishing the principles by which scriptural exegesis should be done. His experimenting with establishing and following stated methods prepares the way for later writings (e.g., *On the Usefulness of Believing; On Christian Teaching*) where his methods become much more secure in his thinking. In this work, Augustine states that there are various ways of interpreting Gen. 1, but that the process for doing so should consist in asking questions and inquiring into the text, rather than making definitive affirmations. Because there have been many heretics who twist the interpretation of Scripture in order to fit their own schemes, Augustine writes, "So before we undertake the study of this book Genesis, we must briefly set out the catholic faith" (1.1).

The version of the faith cited by Augustine is a derivative of the baptismal creed used in the North African churches, based on the Nicene Creed as an interpretive mechanism. But it is obvious that this is a much expanded version of the African Creed for its readers, so that not only its words but also some of its implications may be factored into the task of biblical exegesis.

THE RULE OF FAITH

A. Aristides: Basic Faith (ca. 120–30)

Now the Christians trace their origin from the Lord Jesus Christ. And he is acknowledged by the Holy Spirit to be the Son of the Most High God, who came down from heaven for the salvation of men. And being born of a pure virgin, unbegotten and immaculate, he assumed flesh . . . and tasted death on a cross . . . and after three days, he came to life again and ascended into heaven. (*Apology* 15; *Creeds and Confessions*, 1:52, adapted)

Aristides (of Athens), a little-known apologist of the second century, wrote his *Apology* as an address to the emperor around AD 125 or shortly thereafter, exonerating the views of the Christians from false accusations by giving a true account of what they believe. The passage above provides part of the accepted christological teaching that Aristides claims was the "doctrine of the truth" preached by the apostles and still observed in his day. It is reasonable to suppose that this summary of the Christian tradition was derived from the oral teaching of early second century churches, and that this teaching was presented in a form not unlike the manner stated here.

B. *Epistle of the Apostles:* The Father and Incarnate Word (ca. 150)

We know this: that our Lord and Savior Jesus Christ is God and Son of God, who was sent from God, the Ruler of the entire world, the Maker and Creator of what is named with every name, who is over all authority, Lord of lords and King of kings [1 Tim. 6:15; Rev. 17:14; 19:16], the Ruler of the rulers, the heavenly one who is over the cherubim and seraphim and sits at the right hand of the throne of the Father [Matt. 22:44; 26:64; Acts 2:33], who by his word commanded the heavens and built the earth and its boundaries, and caused deeps and springs to bubble up and flow over the earth day and night; who established the sun, moon, and stars in heaven, who separated light from darkness [Gen. 1:14]; who commanded hell, and in the twinkling of an eye summons the rain for the wintertime, and fog, frost, and hail, and the days in their time; who shakes and makes strong; who has created man according to his image and likeness [Gen. 1:26]; who spoke in parables through the patriarchs and prophets and in truth through him whom the apostles declared and the disciples touched.

And God, the Lord, and the Son of God, we believe: that the Word which became flesh though the Holy Virgin Mary [John 1:14], was hidden in her birth-pangs by the Holy Spirit, and was born not by the lust of flesh but by the will of God [John 1:13], and he was wrapped [in swaddling clothes] and revealed in Bethlehem; and that he was reared and grew up as we saw. (*Epistle of the Apostles* 3; *Creeds and Confessions*, 1:54, slightly modified)

The epistle purports to be a letter composed by the eleven apostles after the ascension of Christ, in which the apostles formally establish their profession of faith. In reality, it is an apocryphal document written long after the apostles' deaths, which is in keeping with quite a number of documents from the second and early third centuries claiming to represent other acts and teachings of the apostles than those found in the New Testament. The above profession, notwithstanding, provides further insight into the christological teaching and profession developing in the second century.

C. Irenaeus of Lyons (ca. 180)

1. The Canon of Truth

The church, though dispersed throughout the whole world, even to the ends of the earth, has received from the apostles and their disciples this faith: she believes in one God, the Father Almighty, Maker of heaven and earth, and the sea, and all things that are in them; and in one Christ Jesus, the Son of God, who became incarnate for our salvation; and in the Holy Spirit, who proclaimed through the prophets the dispensations of God, and the advent, and the birth from a virgin, and the passion, and the resurrection from the dead, and the ascension into heaven, . . . and his future revelation from heaven in the glory of the Father. . . .

The Rule of Truth which we hold, is, that there is one God Almighty, who made all things by His Word, and fashioned and formed, out of that which had no existence, all things that exist. Thus the Scripture says, to that effect, "By the word of the Lord were the heavens established, and all the might of them, by the spirit of his mouth" [Ps. 33:6]. And again, "All things were made by him, and without him was nothing made" [John 1:3]. There is no exception or deduction stated; but the Father made all things by him, whether visible or invisible, objects of sense or of intelligence, temporal, on account of a certain character given them, or eternal; and these eternal things he did not make by angels, or by any powers separated from his Ennoea.[1] For God needs none of all these things, but is he who, by his Word and Spirit, makes, and disposes, and governs all things, and commands all things into existence,—he who formed the world (for the world is of all),—he who fashioned man,—he [who] is the God of Abraham, and the God of Isaac, and the God of Jacob, above whom there is no other God, nor initial principle, nor power. (*Against Heresies* 1.10.1; 1.22.1; *ANF* 1:330, 347, slightly modified)

Several times Irenaeus refers to the Rule of Truth in one form or another in an anti-gnostic work entitled *Against Heresies* (ca. AD 180), where he confronts the Gnostics' claim of possessing secret and authentic teachings of Jesus. Considering on which plane he will refute his adversaries, he is forced to make a distinction between Scripture and tradition since they agree with neither (3.2.2). Even though Irenaeus is eager to show the falsities of the gnostic system through the authority of Scripture, he recognizes that their inconsistent hermeneutics may annul this approach. To illustrate the problem, he asks the reader to envision a beautiful mosaic of a king studded with jewels (i.e., the Bible) which is then perversely dismembered and rearranged to look like a dog or a fox (gnostic interpretations). "In doing so, however, they disregard the order and connection of the Scriptures, destroying the truth" (1.8.1). Irenaeus concludes that one cannot proceed with proofs from Scripture without resorting to a reference outside of it.

2. The Apostolic Preaching

Since it is faith that maintains our salvation, one must take great care of this sustenance to have a true perception of reality. Now

1. "Thought," an aeon in the gnostic scheme of aeons, or beings.

this is what faith does for us, as the elders—the disciples of the apostles—have handed down to us. First of all, it admonishes us to remember that we have received baptism for the remission of sins in the name of God the Father, and in the name of Jesus Christ, the Son of God, who became incarnate and died and was raised, and in the name of the Holy Spirit of God; and that this baptism is the seal of eternal life and is rebirth unto God, that we be no more children of mortals, but of the eternal and everlasting God; and that the eternal and everlasting One is God and is above all creatures, and that all things whatsoever are subject to Him; and that what is subject to Him was all made by Him, so that . . . all things are God's; and that God, therefore, is the Almighty, and all things whatsoever are from God. (*Proof of the Apostolic Preaching* 3; Joseph P. Smith, trans., *Proof of the Apostolic Preaching*, ACW 16 [Westminster, MD: Newman, 1952], 49–50)

It is characteristic of Irenaeus to lay stress on the centrality of the church in the faithful transmission of apostolic teaching. There can be no revelation apart from Scripture and the tradition, and only within the church has this revelation been handed down. It is not merely that the church is the arbitrator of how one should understand and apply the faith, but that the church is the receiver and guardian of that faith through the succession of bishops. For the apostles themselves instituted overseers (i.e., pastors or bishops) in the first churches, and it is through them that the apostolic preaching has come down to the present time.

D. Tertullian of Carthage (ca. 200)

1. Same Rule Taught by Christ

You must know that which prescribes the belief that there is one only God, and that he is none other than the Creator of the world, who produced all things out of nothing through his own Word, first of all things sent forth; that this Word is called his Son, and under the name of God, was seen variously by the patriarchs, heard always in the prophets, at last brought down by the Spirit and Power of the Father into the virgin Mary, was made flesh in her womb, and, being born of her, went forth as Jesus Christ; thenceforth he preached the new law and the new promise of the kingdom of heaven, worked miracles; having been crucified, he rose again on the third day; having ascended into heaven, he sat at the right hand of the Father; sent instead of himself[2] the power

2. Latin *vicariam*.

of the Holy Spirit, who leads the faithful; will come with glory to take the saints to the enjoyment of everlasting life and the celestial promises, and to condemn the wicked to everlasting fire, after a resurrection of both classes has been effected, together with the restoration of the flesh. This rule, as it will be proved, was taught by Christ. (*On the Prescription of Heretics* 13; ANF 3:249, slightly modified)

2. The Economy of Faith in Christ

We believe in one only God, yet subject to this dispensation (which is our word for "economy") that the one only God has also a Son, his Word who has proceeded from himself, by whom all things were made; and without whom nothing has been made: that this Son was sent by the Father into the Virgin and was born of her both man and God, Son of man and Son of God, and was named Jesus Christ: that he suffered, died, and was buried, according to the Scriptures, and, having been raised up by the Father and taken back into heaven, sits at the right hand of the Father and will come to judge the quick and the dead, and that thereafter he, according to his promise, sent from the Father the Holy Spirit the Paraclete, the sanctifier of the faith of those who believe in the Father and the Son and the Holy Spirit. (*Against Praxeas* 2; E. Evans, trans., *Against Praxeas* [London: SPCK, 1948])

Like most of his contemporaries, Tertullian was firm on the point that the Rule of Faith in his time was essentially the same as in the time of the apostles. There certainly are problems with this view, but the Rule was a means of summing up the apostolic message about God's redemption through Christ and sanctification by the Holy Spirit. The term "economy" (or "dispensation") literally means a plan or arrangement. In this case, the economy of God is how the plan of salvation is accomplished in history through the Father, the Son, and the Holy Spirit. Thus, there is an indissoluble relationship between the process of salvation and the existence of the three members of the Trinity. For most of the second and third centuries, the "backbone" of the tradition consisted of an "economical Trinity."

E. Origen of Alexandria: The Apostolic Teaching (ca. 250)

The kind of doctrines which are believed in plain terms through the apostolic teaching are the following:

First that God is one, who created and set in order all things, and who, when nothing existed, caused the universe to be. He is God from the first creation and the foundation of the world, the God of all righteous men, of Adam, Abel, Seth, Enos, Enoch, Noah, Shem, Abraham, Isaac, Jacob, of the twelve patriarchs, of Moses and the prophets. This God, in these last days, according to the previous announcements made through his prophets, sent the Lord Jesus Christ, first for the purpose of calling Israel, and secondly, after the unbelief of the people of Israel, of calling the Gentiles also. This just and good God, the Father of our Lord Jesus Christ, himself gave the Law, the Prophets, and the Gospels, and he is God both of the Apostles and also of the Old and New Testaments.

Then again Christ Jesus, he who came to earth, was begotten of the Father before every created thing. And after he had ministered to the Father in the foundation of all things, for "all things were made through him" [John 1:3], in these last times he emptied himself and was made man, was made flesh, although he was God [Phil 2:7]; and being made man, he still remained what he was, namely, God. He took to himself a body like our body, differing in this alone, that his was born of a virgin and of the Holy Spirit. And this Jesus Christ was born and suffered in truth and not merely in appearance, and truly died our common death. Moreover he truly rose from the dead, and after the resurrection companied with his disciples and was then taken up into heaven.

Then again, the apostles delivered this doctrine, that the Holy Spirit is united in honor and dignity with the Father and the Son. In regard to him it is not yet clearly known whether he is to be thought of as begotten or unbegotten, or as being himself also a Son of God or not; but these matters which we must investigate to the best of our power from the Holy Scripture, inquiring with wisdom and diligence. It is, however, certainly taught with the utmost clearness in the church, that this Spirit inspired each one of the saints, both the prophets and the apostles, and that there was not one Spirit in the men of old and another in those who were inspired at the coming of Christ.

Next after this the apostles taught that the soul, having a substance and life of its own, will be rewarded according to its deserts after its departure from this world; for it will either obtain an inheritance of eternal life and blessedness, if its deeds shall warrant this, or it must be given over to eternal fire and torments, if the guilt of its crimes shall so determine. Further, there will be a time for the resurrection of the dead, when this body, which is now "sown in corruption," shall "rise in incorruption," and that which is "sown in dishonor" shall "rise in glory" [1 Cor. 15:42].

This also is laid down in the church's teaching, that every rational soul is possessed of free will and choice; and also, that it is engaged in a struggle against the devil and his angels and the opposing powers; for these strive to weigh down the soul with sins, whereas we, if we lead a wise and upright life, endeavor to free ourselves from such a burden. There follows from this the conviction that we are not subject to necessity, so as to be compelled by every means, even against our will, to do either good or evil. For if we are possessed of free will, some spiritual powers may very likely be able to urge us on to sin and others to assist us to salvation; we are not, however, compelled by necessity to act either rightly or wrongly, as is thought to be the case by those who say that human events are due to the course and motion of the stars, not only those events which fall outside the sphere of our freedom of will but even those that lie within our own power.

In regard to the soul, whether it takes its rise from the transference of the seed, in such a way that the principle or substance of the soul may be regarded as inherent in the seminal particles of the body itself; or whether it has some other beginning, and whether this beginning is begotten or unbegotten, or at any rate whether it is imparted to the body from without or no; all this is not very clearly defined in the teaching.

Further, in regard to the devil and his angels and the opposing spiritual powers, the church teaching lays it down that these beings exist, but what they are or how they exist it has not explained very clearly. Among most Christians, however, the following opinion is held, that this devil was formerly an angel, but became an apostate and persuaded as many angels as he could to fall away with him; and these are even now called his angels.

The church teaching also includes the doctrine that this world was made and began to exist at a definite time and that by reason of its corruptible nature it must suffer dissolution. But what existed before this world, or what will exist after it, has not yet been made known openly to the many, for no clear statement on the point is set forth in the church teaching.

Then there is the doctrine that the Scriptures were composed through the Spirit of God and that they have not only that meaning which is obvious, but also another which is hidden from the majority of readers. For the contents of Scripture are the outward forms of certain mysteries and the images of divine things. On this point the entire church is unanimous, that while the whole law is spiritual, the inspired meaning is not recognized by all, but only by those who are gifted with the grace of the Holy Spirit in the

word of wisdom and knowledge. (*On First Principles* preface 4–8;
Butterworth, *Origen*, 2–5)

This production of *On First Principles*, written in four books, is among the earliest known attempts to offer a unifying presentation of Christian theology, treating God as Father, the Son in an eternal relation to the Father, the Spirit as unifying, the creation and destruction of the world, the soul, principalities and powers, and the doctrine of Scripture.[3] All these points, on which Origen elaborates, are part of the "definite line and unmistakable rule" laid down by the church.[4] Such teaching is regarded as the "apostolic teaching," in plain terms that all Christians ought to believe. But Origen is also careful to designate those "gray" areas of Christian doctrine that do not share a consensual agreement among churches. He knows there is a difference between the "core" tenets of the faith and those that are more peripheral.

F. Novatian of Rome: Rule of the Creator (ca. 245)

The rule of truth requires that we believe, first in God and Father and Almighty Lord, the most perfect Creator of all things. He suspended the heavens above in their lofty height, made firm the earth with the heavy mass under it, poured forth the freely flowing water of the seas; and he arranged all these, in full abundance and order, with appropriate and suitable essentials.

The same rule of truth teaches us, after we believe in the Father, to believe also in the Son of God, Christ Jesus, the Lord our God, nevertheless the Son of God. We are to believe in the Son of this God who is the one and only God; namely, the Creator of all things, as has already been set forth above.

Next, well-ordered reason and the authority of the faith bid us (in the words and writings of our Lord set down in orderly fashion) to believe, after these things, also in the Holy Spirit, who was in times past promised to the church and duly bestowed at the appointed, favorable moment. (*On the Trinity* 1.1; 9.1; 29.1; *Creeds and Confessions*, 1:69, slightly modified)

Novatian was a presbyter in Rome and diligently sought to preserve the purity of the church's teaching. At some point in his career, this diligence brought him to withhold communion to *traditores*, those who had denied the Christian faith or handed over copies of the Scriptures to persecuting authorities. This ultra-purist approach eventually caused the church to brand Novatian as a schismatic.

3. "Composed through the Spirit of God."
4. *On First Principles*, preface 2.

G. Didascalia Apostolorum: A Christological Benediction (3rd cent.)

Now to him who is able to open the ears of your hearts to receive the incisive words of the Lord through the Gospel and the teaching of Jesus Christ the Nazarene who was crucified in the days of Pontius Pilate, and slept,[5] that he might announce to Abraham, to Isaac and to Jacob and to all his saints the end of the world and the resurrection that is to come for the dead,[6] and rose from the dead, that he might show and give to us, that we might know him, a pledge of his resurrection, and was taken up into heaven by the power of God his Father and of the Holy Spirit, and at the right hand of the throne of God Almighty upon the cherubim, to him who cometh with power and glory to judge both the dead and the living, to him be dominion and glory . . . (*Didascalia Apostolorum* 26; Hanson, *Tradition*, 89)

The so-called *Didascalia* is an artificial title given to an anonymous third-century work known as *The Teaching of the Twelve Apostles and Disciples of Our Savior*. While the original Greek is lost with the exception of a few fragments, the complete work has been recovered in several Syriac translations as well as in later Latin, Ethiopic, and Arabic versions.

H. Augustine

1. What Is to Be Enjoyed by the Christian (ca. 397)

The things that are to be enjoyed[7] are the Father and the Son and the Holy Spirit, in fact, the Trinity; one supreme thing, and one which is shared in common by all who enjoy it. . . . It is not easy, after all, to find any name that will really fit transcendent majesty. In fact, it is better just to say that this Trinity is the one God *from*

5. In death.
6. An oblique reference to 1 Pet. 3:19, 4:6 that Christ preached to the spirits in prison, taken to mean that Christ proclaimed freedom and brought release to the Old Testament saints waiting in Hades for redemption. The apocryphal work known as the *Acts of Pilate* offers a detailed account of Christ's sojourn in hell before his ascension. Later church creeds refer to it as well.
7. Things to be "enjoyed" are the things that we ought to love for their own sake. All other things are to be "used," that is, these things that we enjoy for other ends. Thus, Augustine says, "Among all the things there are, therefore, those alone are to be enjoyed which we have noted as being eternal and unchanging, while the rest are to be used, in order that we may come at last to the enjoyment of the former sort" (*On Christian Teaching* 1.22.20).

whom are all things, in whom are all things [Rom. 11:36]. Thus Father and Son and Holy Spirit are both each one of them singly God and all together one God; and each one of them singly is the complete divine substance, and all together are one substance.

The Father is neither the Son nor the Holy Spirit; the Son is neither the Father nor the Holy Spirit; the Holy Spirit is neither the Father nor the Son; but the Father is only the Father, and the Son only the Son, and the Holy Spirit only the Holy Spirit. The three possess the same eternity, the same unchangeableness, the same greatness, the same power. In the Father unity, in the Son equality, in the Holy Spirit the harmony of unity and equality; and these three are all one because of the Father, are all equal because of the Son, are all linked together because of the Holy Spirit. . . .

That is why, since we are meant to enjoy that truth which is unchangeably alive, and since it is in its light that God the Trinity, author and maker of the universe, provides for all the things he has made, our minds have to be purified, to enable them to perceive that light, and to cling to it once perceived. We should think of this purification process as being a kind of walk, a kind of voyage toward our home country. We do not draw near, after all, by movement in place to the one who is present everywhere, but by honest commitment and good behavior. (*On Christian Teaching* 1.5.5; 1.10.10; *WSA* 1/11:108, 110)

Augustine does not use the actual phrase "Rule of Faith" here. Yet there is no doubt that *On Christian Teaching* 1.5.5–1.21.19 (*WSA* 1/11:108–14) (partially stated above) provides the reader with a creed-like recital of topics central to the faith, beginning with God and moving through the incarnation and the church to the bodily resurrection. In the late fourth and early fifth centuries we find occasional mention of the Rule, though it appears that the notion of the Rule has become more broadly construed than in earlier centuries. Sometimes it is used as representing a summary of the church's faith in the manner of indicating a set of confessional points and sometimes as signifying a hermeneutical principle for rightly interpreting Scripture. In Augustine's *On Christian Teaching*, for example, we find the latter use usually at work; the "Rule," like a set of principles, enables one to read Scripture according to a christological interpretation in harmony with Nicene theology.

2. The Catholic Faith (ca. 421)

What is the certain and distinctive foundation of the catholic faith? You would have the answers to all these questions if you really understood what one should believe, what one should hope for, and what one ought to love.

As this faith begins to penetrate the soul, it changes into sight, through the vital power of goodness, so that the holy and perfect heart catches glimpses of that ineffable beauty,[8] a full vision of whom is our highest happiness. Here, then, is the answer to the question about the beginning and end of our task. We begin in faith, we are perfected in sight [1 Cor. 13:10–11]. This is likewise the most comprehensive of all explanations. As for the certain and distinctive foundation of the catholic faith, it is Christ. (*Enchiridion* 1.4–5; LCC 7:338)

The Rule or "Catholic Faith" guides the inquirer toward the content of the church's faith, hope, and love via the essentials of Christian belief: God as the Creator and Goodness of all creation, the fall of humanity into sin, Jesus Christ the incarnate mediator, the role of the Holy Spirit in the Trinity, baptism and regeneration, the church, forgiveness of sins, the reality of the resurrection, and the life in the world to come. All this Augustine calls "our confession of faith" which is milk for spiritual infants, but food for the strong believer when it is pondered and studied (*Enchiridion* 30.114; LCC 7:407).

I. Vincent of Lérins: The Rule of Doctrine Development (mid–5th cent.)

I have often inquired most earnestly and attentively from very many experts in sanctity and learning, how, and by what definite and, as it were, universal rule I might distinguish the truth of the Catholic Faith from the falsity of heretical perversion; and I have always received an answer of this kind from almost all of them, namely, that whether I, or any one else, wished to detect the frauds of newly rising heretics and to avoid their snares, and to remain sound and whole in the sound faith, one ought, with the Lord's help, to fortify one's faith in a twofold manner: first, by the authority of the Divine Law, and secondly, by the tradition of the Catholic Church.

Here perhaps some one will ask, if the canon of Scripture is complete and is in itself sufficient, and more than sufficient on all points, what need is there to join to it the authority of ecclesiastical interpretation? The answer of course is that, owing to the very depth of holy Scripture itself, all do not receive it in one and the same sense; but one in one way and another in another interprets the declarations of the same writer, so that it seems possible to elicit from it as many opinions as there are men. For Novatian expounds it one way, Photinus another, Sabellius another, Donatus

8. God.

another, Arius, Eunomius, and Macedonius another, Apollinarius and Priscillian another, Jovinian, Pelagius, and Celestius another, and quite lately Nestorius another.[9] Whence it is most necessary, on account of the great intricacies of such various errors, that the rule for the interpretation of the Prophets and Apostles should be laid down in accordance with the standard of the ecclesiastical and Catholic understanding of them.

Also in the Catholic Church itself we take great care that we hold that which has been believed everywhere, always, by all. For that is truly and properly "Catholic," as the very force and meaning of the word show, which comprehends everything almost universally. And we shall observe this rule if we follow universality, antiquity, consent. We shall follow universality if we confess that one Faith to be true which the whole Church throughout the world confesses; antiquity if we in no wise depart from those interpretations which it is plain that our holy predecessors and fathers proclaimed; consent if in antiquity itself we eagerly follow the definitions and beliefs of all, or certainly nearly all, priests and doctors alike.

What if some new contagion seeks to infect the whole Church, and not merely a small portion of it? Then he must take pains to find out and compare the opinions of the ancients, provided, of course, that such remained in the communion and faith of the One Catholic Church, although they lived in different times and places, conspicuous and approved teachers; and whatever he shall find to have been held, written, and taught, not by one or two only, but by all equally and with one consent, openly, frequently and persistently, that he must understand is to be believed by himself also without the slightest hesitation.

But some one will say perhaps, Is there, then, to be no religious progress in Christ's Church? Progress certainly, and that the greatest. For who is he so jealous of others and so odious to God who would attempt to forbid it? . . . For progress implies a growth within the thing itself, while change turns it into something else. Consequently the understanding, knowledge, and wisdom of each and all—and of the whole Church—ought to grow and progress greatly and eagerly through the course of ages and centuries, provided that the advance be within its own lines, in the same sphere of doctrine, the same feeling, the same sentiment. Therefore, whatever has been sown in the Church, which is God's garden, by the fidelity of the Fathers, the same ought to be cultivated and tended by the

9. Names of reputed heretics from the third to the fifth century, not in exact chronological order.

industry of their children, the same ought to flourish and ripen, to advance and be perfected. For it is right that the ancient doctrines of heavenly philosophy should, as time goes on, be carefully tended, smoothed, polished: it is not right for them to be changed, maimed, mutilated. They may gain in evidence, light, distinctness, but they must not lose their completeness, integrity, characteristic property. (*Commonitorium* 2.4–3.8; 23.54, 57–58; *CCC* 322–24)

Baptismal Formulas and Instruction

A. An Early Confession (2nd cent.)

> I believe in God, the Father Almighty,
> And in his only-begotten Son
> Our Lord Jesus Christ,
> And in the Holy Spirit,
> And in the resurrection of the flesh,
> And in the holy catholic church.

> *(Dêr Balyzeh Papyrus,* in Kelly, *Early Christian Creeds,* 88)

Like most confessions, the fundamental components of what makes one's belief specifically Christian is presented in this short formula; it was easy to remember and offered a basic structure for thinking about God. The exact date of the confession is unknown, though its simplicity suggests sometime in the second century.

B. *Apostolic Constitutions:* The Goal of Baptismal Instruction (ca. 4th cent.)

Let him, therefore, who is to be taught the truth in regard to piety be instructed before his baptism in the knowledge of the Unbegot-

ten God, in the understanding of His Only-begotten Son, in the
assured acknowledgement of the Holy Spirit. Let him learn the
order of the several parts of the creation, the series of providential
acts, the different workings of God's laws.

Let him be instructed about why the world was made, and why
man was appointed to be a citizen in it; let him also know about
his own human nature, of what sort of creature he is; let him be
taught how God punished the wicked with water and fire, and
glorified the saints in every generation, . . . and how God did not
reject mankind, but called them from their error and vanity to
acknowledge the truth in various stages of history, leading them
from bondage and impiety to liberty and piety, from injustice to
justice, from death eternal to everlasting life. (*Apostolic Constitutions* 7.39.1–4; *ANF* 7:475–76, slightly altered)

Some of the terms used may be unfamiliar, but the gist of the writer's intention is clear
enough. The new Christian should become acquainted with the truths about God's identity
as Father, Son, and Spirit and confess that the one God is truly a Trinity. It is this God and no
other being or force who made and orders the world, and whose laws have given guidance
throughout history, tailored for each stage. The convert should discover the truth about his
own created nature, that he stands responsible before God for freely following after the good
and the true. The *Apostolic Constitutions* is a composite work edited by an unknown person in
the fourth century, although it contains much material from earlier times.

C. Irenaeus of Lyons: The Three Articles of Our Seal (ca. 180)

God the Father, uncreated, beyond grasp, invisible, one God the
maker of all; this is the first and foremost article of our faith. But
the second article is the Word of God, the Son of God, Christ Jesus
our Lord, who was shown forth by the prophets according to the
design of their prophecy and according to the manner in which the
Father disposed; and through Him were made all things whatsoever.
He also, in the end of times, . . . became a man among men, visible and tangible, in order to abolish death and bring to light life,
and bring about the communion of God and man. And the third
article is the Holy Spirit, through whom the prophets prophesied
and the patriarchs were taught about God, . . . and who in the end
of times has been poured forth in a new manner upon humanity
over all the earth, renewing man to God.

Therefore the baptism of our rebirth comes through these three
articles, granting us rebirth unto God the Father, through the Son,

by the Holy Spirit. (*Proof of the Apostolic Preaching* 3, 6–7; Joseph P. Smith, trans., *Proof of the Apostolic Preaching*, ACW 16 [Westminster, MD: Newman, 1952], 49, 51)

The above is a handbook of catechetical instruction by Irenaeus. A late second-century work, it survives today only in a sixth-century Armenian translation. The addressee of the work, a certain Marcianus, is told that its aim is to "set forth in brief the preaching of the truth" by providing "in brief the proof [or exposition] of the things of God," meaning a concentrated explanation of God's unfolding plan for salvation.

When compared to the Rule of Truth that Irenaeus also mentions in the same chapter of this work (and in *Against Heresies*, see chap. 3.C.1, above), our passage shows the close, sometimes almost indistinguishable, relation between the church's Rule of Faith and the local baptismal formula. Since there was no fixed standard for either the rule or baptismal confessions, it is difficult to see how much the two shared, but they certainly overlapped. Nevertheless, the Rule seemed to have a broader sphere of application and seems to have helped qualify the theological meaning of the baptismal confession. See Augustine's opening statement about the two in section J, below.

The trinitarian pattern, or "three articles," is not fashioned by Irenaeus, but more likely he is incorporating a baptismal confessional form of faith already used in the West at that time. In chapter 100, Irenaeus refers to the above passage as the "three articles of our seal," a clear indication that it was used as part of the prebaptismal instruction.

D. Hippolytus: Baptismal Questions of Affirmation (ca. 215)

When each of them to be baptized has gone down into the water, the one baptizing shall lay hands on each of them, asking,

"Do you believe in God the Father Almighty?"

And the one being baptized shall answer, "I believe."

He shall then baptize each of them once, laying his hand upon each of their heads. Then he shall ask,

"Do you believe in Jesus Christ, the Son of God, who was born of the Holy Spirit and the virgin Mary, who was crucified under Pontius Pilate, and died, and rose on the third day living from the dead, and ascended into heaven, and sat down at the right hand of the Father, the one coming to judge the living and the dead?"

When each has answered, "I believe," he shall baptize a second time.

Then he shall ask,

"Do you believe in the Holy Spirit and the Holy Church and the resurrection of the flesh?"

Then each being baptized shall answer, "I believe." And thus let him baptize the third time.

Prayer of Confirmation

The bishop will then lay his hand upon them, invoking,
saying,
"Lord God, you who have made these worthy
of the removal of sins through the bath of regeneration,
make them worthy to be filled with your Holy Spirit,
grant to them your grace,
that they might serve you according to your will,
for to you is the glory,
Father and Son
with the Holy Spirit,
in the Holy Church,
now and throughout the ages of the ages.
Amen.

(*Apostolic Tradition* 21.12–18; 22.1; based on Gregory Dix,
*The Treatise on the Apostolic Tradition of St. Hippolytus of
Rome, Bishop and Martyr* [London: SPCK, 1937], 37–38)

The *interrogatio* (questioning the candidate) at the time of baptism is from a form of words presumably used in the church at Rome. After a period of instruction and probation that lasted up to three years, a catechumen was baptized, by being first asked to confirm his or her faith while standing in the waters, and by responding to the above questions. This interrogatory format is built on the baptismal formula itself. Other churches did not necessarily use this format, but it was common for all orthodox churches to baptize three times in the names of the Trinity.

E. Gregory Thaumaturgos: A Declaration of Faith (mid–3rd cent.)

Now the words of the initiation are these:
One God: Father of the living Word, subsistent wisdom and power and eternal impress; perfect begetter of perfect; Father of the only-begotten Son [Heb. 1:3].
One Lord: only from only; God from God; impress and image of the Godhead; effective Word; wisdom embracing the structure of the universe, and power which makes the entire creation; true Son of true Father; invisible of invisible, and incorruptible of incorruptible, and immortal of immortal, and eternal of eternal.

One Holy Spirit: holding existence from God, and manifested though the Son (namely, to human beings); perfect image of the perfect Son; life, the cause of living things; holiness who makes sanctification possible; by whom is manifested God the Father, who is over all and in all, and God the Son, who is through all.

Perfect Trinity: in glory and eternity and sovereignty neither divided nor estranged.

Therefore there is nothing created or subservient in the Trinity, nor is anything introduced which did not exist before but came later. Therefore neither did the Son fall short of the Father, nor the Spirit of the Son; but the same Trinity remains always undisturbed and unaltered. (quoted by Gregory of Nyssa, *Sermons* 10.1; FOC 98:54)

Since these words are recorded by Gregory of Nyssa, it is uncertain how much of the declaration actually originated from the other Gregory. Gregory Thaumaturgos was a close pupil of Origen and became bishop of Neocaesarea in Pontus (ca. AD 240), which is where the formula may have been used. There is nothing in the wording that prevents the above from being dated to the mid-third century.

F. Egeria: Scripture Interpreted for Those to Be Baptized (later 4th cent.)

I must write something about how the ones who are baptized at Easter are instructed. Now he who gives in his name, gives it in on the day before Quadragesima,[1] and the priest writes down the names of all; this is before the eight weeks which I have said are kept here at Quadragesima.

And when the priest has written down the names of all, after the next day of Quadragesima, that is, on the day when the eight weeks begin, the chair is set for the bishop in the midst of the great church, that is, at the martyrium, and the priests sit in chairs on either side of him, while all the clergy stand. Then one by one the *competentes*[2] are brought up, coming, if they are males with their fathers, and if females with their mothers.

1. The first Sunday of Lent, a forty-day period from Ash Wednesday to Easter. Egeria is observing that the eight weeks of the custom in the East is the same as the Western custom of keeping forty days. The Eastern count does not include Saturdays and Sundays.
2. Learners, or those catechumens who have reached the final stage in their preparation, continue the Lenten period with a more intensive period of instruction and self-examination.

Then the bishop asks the neighbors of every one who has entered concerning each individual, saying: "Does this person lead a good life, being obedient to the parents, and not given to wine, nor deceitful?" He also makes inquiry about the several vices that are more serious among men and women.

And if he has proved him in the presence of witnesses to be blameless in all these matters concerning which he has made inquiry, he writes down his name with his own hand. But if he is accused in any matter, he orders him to go out, saying: "Let him amend, and when he has amended, then let him come to the font."[3] And as he makes inquiry concerning the men, so also does he concerning the women. But if any be a stranger, he comes not so easily to baptism, unless he has testimonials from those who know him.

The custom here is that those who come to baptism through those forty days, which are kept as fast days, are first exorcised by the clergy early in the day, as soon as the morning dismissal has been made in the Anastasis.[4] Immediately afterward the chair is placed for the bishop at the martyrium in the great church, and all who are to be baptized sit around, near the bishop, both men and women, their fathers and mothers standing there also. Besides these, all the people who wish to hear come in and sit down—the faithful only, however.

No catechumen enters there when the bishop teaches the others the Law. Beginning from Genesis he goes through all the Scriptures during those forty days, explaining them, first literally,[5] and then unfolding them spiritually.[6] They are also taught about the resurrection, and likewise all things concerning the faith during those days. And this is called the catechesis.[7]

Then when five weeks are completed from the time when their teaching began, (the *competentes*) are then taught the Creed.[8] And as he [the bishop] explained the meaning of all the Scriptures, so does he explain the meaning of the Creed;[9] each article first literally

3. *Lavacrum.*

4. Originally built by Constantine over the reputed place of Christ's tomb, it was known as the Church of the Holy Sepulchre or the Basilica of the Anastasis ("resurrection" in Greek).

5. Literally or historically interpreting the text.

6. Allegorically and figuratively interpreting the text. This took greater spiritual discernment than the literal and was considered necessary for adequately understanding scriptural meaning.

7. *Catēchēsis*, a Greek word, means "instruction," and those who receive this instruction are called catechumens.

8. Literally, the *Symbol* (= Creed), that which is "handed over" (*traditio*).

9. That is, the Creed of Jerusalem. "Symbol" was the Greek equivalent for the Latin "Creed."

and then spiritually. By this means all the faithful in these parts follow the Scriptures when they are read in church, inasmuch as they are all taught during those forty days from the first to the third hour, for the catechizing lasts for three hours.

And God knows, reverend sisters, that the voices of the faithful who come in to hear the catechizing are louder (in approval) of the things spoken and explained by the bishop than they are when he sits and preaches in church. Then, after the dismissal of the catechizing is made, it being already the third hour, the bishop is at once escorted with hymns to the Anastasis. So the dismissal takes place at the third hour. Thus are they taught for three hours a day for seven weeks, but in the eighth week of Quadragesima, which is called the Great Week, there is no time for them to be taught, because the things that are above must be carried out.

And when the seven weeks are past, the Paschal week is still to come, which they call here the Great Week. Then the bishop comes in the morning into the great church at the martyrium, and the chair is placed for him in the apse behind the altar, where they come one by one, a man with his father and a woman with her mother, and recite the Creed[10] to the bishop.

And when they have recited the Creed to the bishop, he addresses them all, and says: "During these seven weeks you have been taught all the law of the Scriptures; you have also heard concerning the Faith, and concerning the resurrection of the flesh, and the whole meaning of the Creed, as far as you were able, being yet catechumens. But the teachings of the deeper mystery, that is, of baptism itself, you cannot hear, being as yet catechumens. But, lest you should think that anything is done without good reason, these, when you have been baptized in the Name of God, you shall hear in the Anastasis, during the eight Paschal days, after the dismissal from the church has been made. You, being as yet catechumens, cannot be told the more secret mysteries of God."

But when the days of Easter have come, during those eight days, that is, from Easter to the Octave, when the dismissal from the church has been made, they go with hymns to the Anastasis. Prayer is said at that point, the faithful are blessed, and the bishop stands, leaning against the inner rails that are in the cave of the Anastasis, and explains all things that are done in baptism.

In that hour no catechumen approaches the Anastasis, but only the neophytes[11] and the faithful, who wish to hear concerning the myster-

10. Literally, "the handing back" (*redditio*) of the Creed.
11. Newly baptized.

ies, enter there, and the doors are shut lest any catechumen should draw near. And while the bishop discusses and sets forth each point, the voices of those who applaud are so loud that they can be heard outside the church. And truly the mysteries are so unfolded that there is no one unmoved at the things that he hears to be so explained.

Now, forasmuch as in that province some of the people know both Greek and Syriac, while some know Greek alone and others only Syriac; and because the bishop, although he knows Syriac, yet always speaks Greek, and never Syriac, there is always a priest standing by who, when the bishop speaks Greek, interprets into Syriac, that all may understand what is being taught.

And because all the lessons that are read in the church must be read in Greek, he always stands by and interprets them into Syriac, for the people's sake, that they may always be edified. Moreover, the Latins here, who understand neither Syriac nor Greek, in order that they be not disappointed, have (all things) explained to them, for there are other brothers and sisters knowing both Greek and Latin, who translate into Latin for them.

But what is above all things very pleasant and admirable here, is that the hymns, the antiphons,[12] and the lessons, as well as the prayers which the bishop says, always have suitable and fitting references, both to the day that is being celebrated and also to the place where the celebration is taking place. (*The Pilgrimage of Egeria* 45–47; adapted from R. Wilkerson, *Egeria's Travels to the Holy Land*, rev. ed. [Warminster, UK: Aris & Phillips, 1981], 143–46)

Egeria's *Pilgrimage* is a unique narrative from the late fourth century about a woman's travels to Jerusalem, Egypt, and Asia Minor. Her account is fragmented (the beginning is lost), but from what survives we learn much about the state of monasticism, the location of churches, and Christian worship practices in the Middle East at this time. This was true especially of the church of Jerusalem, where Egeria visited more than once and was there for Easter, explaining in detail the services and churches in the city. She spent a period of three years traveling in the area, visiting a multitude of sites mentioned in the Bible and carefully recording her experiences.

G. Cyril of Jerusalem: A Basic Guide for New Christians (ca. 350)

Of God. Let there, then, be laid as first foundation in your souls the dogma concerning God, that God is one alone, unbegotten,

12. Verses or passages sung alternately.

without beginning, unchanging and unchangeable, neither looking to any other as the author of his being, nor to any other to succeed to his life, of which life he had no beginning in time, nor will it ever come to an end. Now this Father of our Lord Jesus Christ is not circumscribed to some place, nor is the arch of heaven beyond him, but "the heavens are the work of his fingers" [Ps. 8:3], and "the whole earth is held in the hollow of his hand" (Isa. 40:12). He is in everything and yet nothing contains him. Do not imagine that God is smaller than the sun, or that he is as large as the sun. For, as he made the sun, he must have been already incomparably greater than the sun, and more resplendent than light. He knows everything, and does as he wills. He is not subject to any law of sequence, or genesis, or fortune, or fate; he is perfect by every measure. He possesses unchangeably every kind of virtue, never less and never more, but ever in the same degree and manner.

Of Christ. Believe also in the Son of God, who is one and only, our Lord Jesus Christ, God begotten from God, life begotten from life, light engendered from light, like in all things to him that begat him:[13] who did not receive his being in time but was begotten of the Father before all ages in a manner eternal and incomprehensible. He is God's wisdom and power and his righteousness existing hypostatically. He is enthroned at God's right hand from before all ages. For he was not, as some have supposed, crowned after his passion, as though God seated him at his right hand for his endurance of the cross, but has royal dignity from that source from which he has his being, namely, he is eternally begotten from the Father, and shares the Father's throne, being God, and, as we said, being the wisdom and power of God. He reigns together with the Father, and through the Father is creator of all things. He falls in nothing short of the Divine majesty and knows the Father that begat him as he himself is known of his Father.

Of Christ's birth of a virgin. You must believe that this only-begotten Son of God came down from heaven to this earth because of our sins, and took upon him manhood of like passions with ours, by being born of the Holy Virgin and of the Holy Spirit, and this incarnation was not docetic[14] or imaginary, but true incarnation. He did not pass through the Virgin as though passing through a channel, but his flesh grew truly from her flesh and he was truly fed

13. For the first half of the fourth century, the relation of the Son to the Father as *homoios* (like) was common to the theology of many, if not most, Eastern bishops instead of the Nicene terminology of *homoousios* (same substance).

14. That Christ seemed or appeared to be physical but was not in reality.

upon her milk. He truly ate as we eat, and drank as we drink. For if the incarnation was but seeming, then did it but seem to bring salvation. Christ was twofold. As for his visibility, he was man, and as for his invisibility, he was God. As man, he ate as genuinely as we do, for he had the same fleshly needs as we have, but as God he made five loaves to feed five thousand men. As man he truly died, and as God, on the third day, he raised to life his body that was dead. As man he was really asleep in the boat, while, as God, he came walking upon the waters.

Of the cross. Christ was truly crucified for our sins. Even supposing you were disposed to contest this, your surroundings rise up before your eyes to refute you, this so cruel Golgotha where we have now come together because of him who was crucified here. Yes, and the wood of the cross is henceforth here and there distributed all over the world. Now, he is not crucified for sins which he had done, but to free us from the sins that are wholly ours. And though he was, at that time, scorned of men, and as man smitten on the face, creation recognized him to be God. But when the sun saw its master being dishonored, it shuddered and ceased to shine, not bearing to see the sight.

In the tomb. Christ was truly, as man, laid in a tomb in the rock, but for dread of him the rocks were rent asunder. He went down to regions under the earth to redeem from thence the righteous. Or, tell me, do you want the living to enjoy the grace of God, and that when the most of them are not deeply religious, and are you quite content that those that have been so long while imprisoned, even from Adam down, should never come to deliverance?[15] Isaiah the prophet with clarion voice proclaimed so many things of Christ. Would you not have the King go down and redeem his herald? David and Samuel were down there, and all the prophets, including John, who sent and asked him, "Are you the one that should come, or do we look for another?"

Of Christ's resurrection. But he that descended beneath the earth came up again from there, and Jesus who was buried, truly rose again on the third day. Now should Jews ever try to pull your faith to pieces, counter them instantly by asking thus: Jonah came forth from the whale after three days, and do you then say that it is not true that Christ rose from the earth after three days? A corpse that touched the bones of Elisha came to life again, and will you argue that he who made men could not more easily than that be

---

15. A reference to Christ descending into Hades before his resurrection, where he freed the Old Testament saints (cf. 1 Pet. 3:19; 4:6).

raised up by the power of God? So, then, Christ truly rose again, and after his resurrection was seen once more by the disciples. Twelve disciples were witnesses of his resurrection, and the measure of their witness is not their winning speech, but their striving for the truth of the resurrection unto torture and to death. Well, now, "at the mouth of two or three witnesses shall every word be established," Scripture says. But those who bore witness to the resurrection of Christ were a round dozen. And after that are you going to find the resurrection incredible?

Of Christ received up. When Jesus had run the course of his endurance, and redeemed men from their sins, he ascended up again into the heavens and a cloud received him from sight. Angels stood by as he ascended, while apostles gazed. If anyone does not credit these words, let him believe simply in virtue of the things he sees today. In the case of every monarch that dies, his power is extinguished in the same breath as his life. But Christ is no sooner crucified than he begins to be worshipped by the whole universe. We preach the crucified, and see, the demons tremble. Many have been the victims of crucifixion through the ages, but of which of them but of him did the invocation ever drive off the demons?

So let us not be ashamed of the cross of Christ, but though someone else keeps it secret, you should openly sign it on your forehead, so that evil spirits beholding the royal emblem may flee far from you in terror. Make this sign as you eat and drink, when you sit down, when you go to bed, when you get up again, while you are talking, while you are walking; in brief, at your every undertaking [cf. Deut. 6:4–9]. He who was crucified then is now in heaven above. For we would have a reason to be ashamed if, after he had been crucified and entombed, he had remained entombed. But now, he who was crucified on this very Golgotha ascended to heaven from the Mount of Olives there to the east. For from hence he went down into Hades and came again to us here. Again he went up from us into heaven, when the Father called him saying, "Sit on my right hand, until I make your enemies your footstool."

Of judgment to come. This ascended Jesus Christ is coming again, from heaven, and not from anywhere on earth. I say "not from anywhere on earth," since there are going to be many antichrists now arising on earth. For, as you have beheld, many have already begun to say, I am Christ. Besides, "the abomination of desolation" is still to come, giving himself the usurped title of Christ. But I urge you to look for the true Christ, the only-begotten Son of God coming, but from heaven, and never again from anywhere on earth; appearing to all more clearly than any lightning, or any brilliance of light, escorted by angels, to judge the living and the dead and reign as king, in a heavenly and eternal kingdom that knows no end. In that point also I bid you make sure your faith; since many are saying that the kingdom of Christ has an end.

Of the Holy Spirit. Also you must believe in the Holy Spirit and possess the right knowledge about him, seeing that there are many who are alien to the Holy Spirit and teach a doctrine concerning him that is no better than blasphemy. But I urge you to learn that this Holy Spirit is one and indivisible, but of manifold powers. Many are his activities, but he himself is not parceled out among them. He knows all mysteries, and "searches all things, even the deep things of God." He descended upon our Lord Jesus Christ in the form of a dove. He wrought in the Law and in the Prophets. And it is this Holy Spirit that seals your soul now, when the time of your baptism comes. Every intelligible nature has need of sanctification from him. If any dare blaspheme against the Holy Spirit, he has no forgiveness, "either in this world, or in that which is to come." In honor he is honored with the majesty of the Father and the Son. Thrones and dominions, principalities and powers, depend on him. For there is one God the Father of Christ, and one Lord Jesus Christ the only-begotten Son of God, and one Holy Spirit, who sanctifies all and makes divine, who spoke in the Law and in the Prophets, in the old covenant and in the new. (*Catechetical Lectures* 4.4–16; LCC 4:100–108)

These baptismal lectures that have survived from Cyril of Jerusalem provide us with a rare glimpse into the confessional and theological life of the Jerusalem church (mid-fourth century). Some eighteen lectures or addresses are recorded which were delivered to baptismal candidates in explanation of the creed, which Cyril asserts to be "the holy and apostolic faith" of Jerusalem.

H. Ambrose of Milan

1. Baptismal Creed of Milan (ca. 385)

I believe in God the Father almighty;

And in Jesus Christ His only Son our Lord, Who was born from the Holy Spirit and (or from) the Virgin Mary, suffered under Pontius Pilate, was crucified and buried, on the third day rose again from the dead, ascended to heaven, sits at the right hand of the Father;

From there he will come to judge the living and the dead;

And in the Holy Spirit, the holy Church, the remission of sins, the resurrection of the flesh. (Kelly, *Early Christian Creeds*, 173)

2. A Glossed[16] Version of the Baptismal Faith (ca. 388)

Here is the Symbol: I BELIEVE . . . [HIS] ONE ONLY, OUR LORD. Thus say: HIS ONE ONLY SON. Is there not but one Lord? There is but one God and but one Lord. But lest they raise accusations against us and say (that we speak of) one Person, let us say that the Son likewise is ONE ONLY, OUR LORD. Since I have spoken of the Divinity of the Father and of the Son, we come now to his incarnation.

WHO WAS BORN [suffered] AND WAS BURIED: here you have the passion and the burial.

THE THIRD DAY [rose again] FROM THE DEAD: here you have his resurrection also.

HE ASCENDED [into the heavens]; SITS AT THE RIGHT HAND OF THE FATHER: You see then that the flesh could in no way impair his Divinity: rather, through the incarnation a great triumph was secured for Christ. For why, when he has ascended from death, does he SIT AT THE RIGHT HAND OF THE FATHER? As one who presents to the Father the fruit of his good pleasure. You have two statements: HE ROSE AGAIN FROM death, he sits AT THE RIGHT HAND OF THE FATHER. In no way therefore could the flesh cause any detriment to the glory of his Divinity.[17]

Hear, what you ought indeed [to] be ready to believe. Faith itself proceeds from love. He who loves never undermines another; a friend who loves his friend never undermines him: much more one who loves the Lord ought not to undermine Him by detracting anything from Him.[18] I tell you why: HE SITS [AT THE RIGHT HAND OF THE FATHER]. . . . Is there not one judgment of the Father and of the Son and of the Holy Spirit? Is there not one will? Is there not one majesty? Why else are you told that the Son is about to judge, except that you may understand that there is to be no detracting the Son?

16. Any text accompanied by explanatory remarks or interpretive instruction.

17. Ambrose's concern is that any weakness of suffering should be attributed to the physical nature of the incarnate Son and not his divine nature or power. Even the concept that Christ was elevated to the right hand of the Father implies that the Son has been in lower position in relation to the Father's divinity—a point that our author here wants to clarify as an erroneous interpretation of the creed.

18. The idea again is that the believer's love of Christ will not lead the believer to suppose that the divine person of Christ is anything less than the divinity of the Father.

See then, you believe in the Father, you believe in the Son; and what in the third place? AND IN THE HOLY SPIRIT. Whatever sacraments you are to receive, you will receive them in this Trinity, let no one mislead you. You see then the venerable Trinity, of one operation, of one sanctification, of one majesty.[19]

But we also claim belief in THE CHURCH; but it has also in THE FORGIVENESS OF SINS; but it has also in THE RESURRECTION. Why is this? The reason is one and the same: as we so believe in Christ, we so also believe in the Father, even as we believe in THE CHURCH and in THE FORGIVENESS OF SINS and in THE RESURRECTION OF THE FLESH.

What is the reason? Because he who believes in the Author believes also in the work of the Author. And now, that you may not imagine this to be a conceit of my own, take a testimony: "If you believe not me, believe at least the works." So you have got that. Your faith will now shine forth the more if you are ready to put full and complete trust in the work of your Author. In HOLY CHURCH and in THE FORGIVENESS OF SINS: believe therefore with faith that all your sins are forgiven. Why? You have read in the Gospel the saving of the Lord: "Thy faith has made you whole" [Mark 10:52; forgiveness of sins], THE RESURRECTION [of the flesh]: believe that the flesh will rise again. For what need was there that Christ should take flesh, what need that Christ should ascend the cross, what need that Christ should taste death, receive burial and rise again, except for the sake of your resurrection? This whole sacrament is concerned with your resurrection. "If Christ rose not again, our faith is vain" [1 Cor. 15:17]; but because he did rise again, our faith stands firm. (*Explanation of the Symbol*; 8–9; Connolly, *Explanatio*, 55, minor alteration)

Besides the many political and ecclesiastical achievements for which he was known, Ambrose had a strong pastoral side that was apparent in his sermons and letters. Part of his pastoral task, in keeping with the episcopal role, was involved with teaching recent converts the fundamentals of the faith. This was the first opportunity the bishop had to impress new Christians with the importance of orthodoxy and the church's role in preserving it. Indeed, Ambrose defines the Symbol as "a spiritual seal, which Symbol is our heart's meditation and as it were an ever-present guard, surely our heart's treasure."

19. This kind of pro-Nicene theology will later be manifested most eloquently by Augustine. The Father does not function in one way while the Son functions in another way and the Spirit still operates in a third and different way. If the Father, Son, and Spirit are of one substance (per Nicaea), then they act jointly in all operations and share in equal majesty and power.

I. Rufinus of Aquileia: Creed of Aquileia (early 5th cent.)

I believe in God the Father Almighty of things visible and invisible,

And in Christ Jesus, His only Son our Lord,
  who was born of the Holy Spirit by the virgin Mary,
  was crucified under Pontius Pilate,
  and buried.
  He descended into the lower places,
  on the third day he arose from the dead,
  he ascended into heaven,
  where he sits on the right hand of the Father.
  From there he will come to judge the living and the dead.

And in the Holy Spirit, the holy church,
  the forgiveness of sins, the resurrection of the flesh.

(Commentary on the Apostles' Creed; Kelly, *Early Christian
Creeds*, 174, adapted)

Rufinus's citation of the creed here is actually the first full appearance of the Apostles' Creed, though it is clearly an offspring of the old Roman Creed, which had long been in circulation in varying forms. Just as the churches of Milan, Ravenna, Turin and others did, Rufinus is using a version of the creed that has been slightly altered for its use in Aquileia. And like the other churches, Rufinus shared the conviction that the creed was the very reflection of what the apostles taught because each of them had a hand in its composition.

J. Augustine: The Baptismal Symbol of Hippo Regius (early 5th cent.)

A Symbol is a briefly compiled rule of faith, intended to instruct the mind without overburdening the memory, and to be said in a few words, from which much is gained. So it is called a "Symbol," because it is something by which Christians can recognize each other. This is what I shall first briefly recite to you.

I believe in God the Father almighty; and in Jesus Christ his only Son, our Lord, who was born of the Holy Spirit and the virgin Mary; under Pontius Pilate crucified and buried, on the third day he rose again from the dead; he ascended into heaven; he is seated at the right hand of the Father, from there to come to judge the living and the dead; and in the Holy Spirit; in the holy Church; in the forgiveness of sins; in the resurrection of the flesh. (*Sermon 213* 2; *WSA* 3/6:141)

The creed is reconstructed from the same sermon that was preached to catechumens in his church of Hippo Regius. Compare this form with the (reconstructed) North African Creed found in Augustine's *On Faith and the Creed* (ca. 392):

I believe in God the Father Almighty, and in Jesus Christ, the Son of God, only-begotten of the Father, our Lord, who was born through the Holy Spirit of the Virgin Mary; who was crucified under Pontius Pilate and buried. On the third day he rose from the dead, ascended into heaven, sits at the right hand of the Father, whence he will come and will judge the living and the dead; and [I believe] in the Holy Spirit, the holy church, the remission of sins, [and] the resurrection of the flesh. (author translation)

K. The "Nicene Creed" for Worship (6th cent.)

We believe in one God, Father Almighty,
Maker of heaven and earth,
of all things visible and invisible.
And [we believe] in one Lord, Jesus Christ, the son of God only-
     begotten,
begotten of the Father before all ages,
Light from Light, True God from True God,
begotten, not made,
of one substance with the Father,
by whom all things were made,
who, for us men and for our salvation,
came down from heaven,
and was made flesh by the Holy Spirit and Mary the virgin,
and became man.
He was crucified under Pontius Pilate,
and suffered, and was buried, and rose again on the third day,
     according to the Scriptures,
and he ascended to heaven,
and sits on the right hand of the Father,
and will come again with glory to judge the living and the dead,
whose kingdom will never end.
And [we believe] in one Holy Spirit, the Lord and Giver of life,
who proceeds from the Father,

who with the Father and Son is together glorified and worshipped, who spoke through the prophets.
And [we believe] in one holy, catholic, and apostolic church.
We confess one baptism
for the forgiveness of sins.
We look for the resurrection of the dead
and the life of the world to come. Amen.

> (author translation; Greek text in O. Montevecchi, "Il Simbolo constantinopolitano in una tavola lignea della collezione dell'Università Cattolica di Milano," *Aegyptus* 55 [1975]: 60–61)

The creed translated was discovered on a wooden tablet (38.5 cm x 19.5 cm) that seems to have been used in an Eastern church in preparing the catechumens for baptism. Although identified as the "Nicene Creed," versions of the Niceno-Constantinopolitan Creed (381) became used as baptismal formulas by the sixth century (see chap. 5.B.5, below). It is the only known case of a creed being written in wood for obvious instructive purposes and almost completely preserved.

Local and Conciliar Creeds

A. Church Creeds

These creeds were indigenous to the local church and often used at baptism. The authority attributed to local creeds was grounded on their venerable connection to the apostolic faith, and on the year-after-year practice of hearing and reciting them in worship and baptismal instruction. Conciliar creeds from Nicaea and Constantinople are clearly distinguished as having another origin, which provided an interpretive mechanism for defining contemporary parameters of orthodoxy and heresy. They were not meant to replace the baptismal confessions since the latter were still regarded as the sacramental norms of the Christian faith.

1. The Creed of Caesarea (3rd cent.)

We believe in One God, Father Almighty, Maker of all things visible and invisible;

And in one Lord Jesus Christ, the Word of God, God from God, Light from Light, Life from Life, Only-begotten Son, first-born of creation, begotten of the Father before all ages, by whom all things were made; who for our salvation was incarnate, and lived among men, and suffered, and rose again on the third day, and ascended to the Father, and will come again in glory to judge the living and the dead.

And in one Holy Spirit. (Stevenson and Frend, *New Eusebius*, 347)

Cited by Eusebius of Caesarea in a letter he wrote to his congregation just after the close of the Nicene Council (325). His intent was to show the close proximity of the Nicene (see B.1, below) and the Caesarean creeds. The fact that he cites the Caesarean church creed as an established creed, older than the Nicene Creed (325), makes it probable that it dates from the previous century.

2. The Jerusalem Creed (early 4th cent.)

We believe in one God, the Father Almighty, maker of heaven and earth, of all things visible and invisible;

And in one Lord Jesus Christ, the only-begotten Son of God, who was begotten of the Father as true God, only-begotten before all ages, by whom all things were made; who appeared in the flesh, and became man; who was crucified and buried and rose again from the dead on the third day, and ascended to heaven, and sat down on the right hand of the Father, and will come again in glory to judge the living and the dead, of whose kingdom there will be no end;

And in one Holy Spirit, the Paraclete, who spoke in the prophets, and in one baptism of repentance for the remission of sins; and in one holy catholic church, and in the resurrection of the flesh, and in the life everlasting.

Learn the faith and profess it; receive it and keep it—but only the Creed which the church will now deliver to you, that Creed is firmly based on Scripture. . . . For the articles of the Creed were not put together according to human choice; the most important doctrines were collected from the whole of Scripture to make up a single exposition of the faith. (*Catechetical Lectures* 5.12; LCC 4:124)

Though it is not found as a separately existing text, the Jerusalem Creed has been culled and reconstructed from Cyril's catechetical lectures (per Kelly, *Early Christian Creeds*, 183–84). Like the Caesarean Creed, the first citation of the Jerusalem Creed is mid–fourth century, but it probably dates back to the previous century.

True to the catechetical nature of these addresses, Cyril's intention was to show the new believers that the creed (of Jerusalem) represented "the holy and apostolic faith." But it was no less a *de facto* summarization of the Scriptures. Indeed, one of the main purposes of learning the creed, he says, is because it represents an epitome of the whole Bible.

LOCAL AND CONCILIAR CREEDS

3. An Alexandrian Statement of Faith (early 4th cent.)

We believe in one unbegotten God, Father Almighty,
maker of all things both visible and invisible,
who has his being from himself;

and in one only-begotten Word, Wisdom, Son,
eternally begotten of the Father without beginning;
a Word that is not [merely] spoken,
nor a mental image, nor a effluence of the Father, nor a dividing of the Unchangeable Essence,
but absolutely perfect Son, living and powerful [Heb. 4:12],
the true image of the Father,
equal in honor and glory, . . . very God of very God, . . . Almighty of Almighty,
Whole from Whole, being like[1] the Father,
as the Lord says, "He that has seen me has seen the Father" [John 14:9].

We believe, likewise, in the Holy Spirit, who "searches all things,
even the deep things of God" [1 Cor. 2:10].

(Exposition of the Faith 1; NPNF 2/4:84–85, adapted)

The author may be Athanasius, though it is difficult to date the text with any precision. An absence of anti-Arian statements suggests that it is earlier than Athanasius's later anti-Arian treatises, which come out of the 340s–350s. Also, the untroubled use of the word "like" for expressing the Son's relation to the Father implies that the author, while espousing a theology of the Nicene Creed, does not feel compelled to track all the language of the creed.

4. Early Roman Creed

I believe in God the Father Almighty;

and in Christ Jesus His only Son, our Lord,
who was born of the Holy Spirit and the virgin Mary,
who under Pontius Pilate was crucified and buried,
on the third day rose again from the dead,
ascended into heaven,

---

1. *Homoios*. A common way of referring to the relation of the Son to the Father before and after the Council of Nicaea. Athanasius prefers to use this term until the 350s.

sits at the right hand of the Father,
whence he will come to judge the living and the dead;

and in the Holy Spirit,
the holy church,
the remission of sins,
the resurrection of the flesh.

(Kelly, *Early Christian Creeds*, 102)

Known as the Old Roman Creed, this formula of faith is the ancestor of the received form of the Apostles' Creed (below) and echoes the interrogatory form of the baptismal faith expressed in the *Apostolic Tradition* (see chap. 4.D, above). A Greek version of the creed, almost identical, was offered in 340 by Marcellus of Ancyra when he wished to defend his orthodoxy for Julius of Rome. But he is not an independent source since he was likely offering a translated version of the Latin creed.

5. The Apostles' Creed (Received Text) (6th cent.)

I believe in God the Father Almighty,
Maker of heaven and earth;

And in Jesus Christ, His only Son, our Lord,
who was conceived by the Holy Spirit,
born of the virgin Mary,
suffered under Pontius Pilate,
was crucified, dead and buried,
descended into hell,
on the third day rose again from the dead,
ascended into heaven,
sits at the right hand of God the Father Almighty,
thence he will come to judge the living and the dead.

I believe in the Holy Spirit,
the holy catholic church,
the communion of saints,
the remission of sins,
the resurrection of the flesh,
and eternal life. Amen.

A uniquely Western creed, the above formula, though with minor differences, is found as early as Rufinus of Aquileia in his *Commentary on the Apostles' Creed* (ca. 404). By the later fourth century, numerous versions of the so-called Apostles' Creed could be found circulating throughout Western Europe. In fact, we might say that the most notable thing about the creed at this time was its diversity. While there were hundreds of different forms of the Apostles' Creed, no two forms were exactly identical. However, in different regions (Gaul, North Italy, Africa, etc.), the creed did share certain regional similarities, eventually congealing by the late sixth century into the textus receptus.

6. Use of the Apostles' Creed in a Prayer (late 5th cent.)

He was born of the virgin Mary, was crucified by Pontius Pilate, and was buried in a tomb; on the third day he arose, was taken up to heaven, and . . .

Jesus, because you healed at that time[2] every sickness and every disease of the people, . . . because you went at that time into the house of Peter's mother-in-law, who was suffering from fever [Mark 1:30–31; Matt. 8:14–16; Luke 4:38–39], and the fever left her. So now we ask you, Jesus, heal also now your servant, who wears your holy name, from every disease, every fever, every shivering fit and every headache,[3] as well as from all bewitching and every evil spirit; in the name of the Father, Son and Holy Spirit. (G. H. R. Horsley, ed., *New Documents Illustrating Early Christianity: A Review of the Greek Inscriptions and Papyri Published in 1978*, New Documents Illustrating Early Christianity 3 [North Ryde, N.S.W.: Ancient History Documentary Research Centre, Macquarie University, 1983], 115)

This is a partially preserved invocation to Christ in the name of the Trinity for healing, drawing on the Apostles' Creed. It is found on a narrow piece of papyrus in Egypt (Papyrus Turner 49) and calls on God in a manner similar to that of religious amulets that contain lines from the Niceno-Constantinopolitan Creed as a means of warding off illness. The use of amulets continued among some Christians despite the frequent opposition voiced against it.

7. Augustine: North African Creed (ca. 392)

I believe in God the Father Almighty,

And in Jesus Christ, the Son of God, only-begotten of the Father, our Lord, who was born through the Holy Spirit of the Virgin Mary; who was crucified under Pontius Pilate and buried. On the third day he rose from the dead, ascended into heaven, sits at the right hand of the Father, whence he will come and will judge the living and the dead;

2. At the time of Christ's earthly ministry, as mentioned by the Gospel account.
3. The translation "headache" is uncertain due to the fragmentary nature of the text.

And [I believe] in the Holy Spirit, the holy church, the remission of sins, [and] the resurrection of the flesh. (*On Faith and the Creed*; J. Burleigh, trans., *Augustine: Earlier Writings* [Philadelphia: Westminster, 1953])

This creed is reconstructed from an exposition of the faith that Augustine delivered to an assembly of North African bishops. Because it is reconstructed, we cannot know the exact wording, but it seems nearly identical to the Milanese creed, according to which Augustine was baptized by Ambrose in 386. Like Aquileia, Ravenna, and other churches, the church creeds in North Africa exhibit many similarities to the Roman Creed.

8. Quodvultdeus: Creed of Carthage (ca. 435)

We believe in God the Father Almighty, creator of the universe,
    And in His Son Jesus Christ, who was born of the Holy Spirit from the Virgin Mary, crucified under Pontius Pilate and buried. On the third day he rose from the dead; He was assumed into heaven, where He sits at the right hand of the Father, from whence he will come to judge the living and the dead.
    And [we believe] in the Holy Spirit, in the remission of [all] sins, in the resurrection of the flesh, in eternal life, through the holy church. (reconstructed from Quodvultdeus's catechetical sermons as presented in *Quodvultdeus of Carthage: The Creedal Homilies*, trans. T. M. Finn, ACW 60 (Mahwah, NJ: Newman, 2004)

Little is known about Quodvultdeus except that he was a younger contemporary of Augustine and became bishop of Carthage around 437, about two years before the city was invaded and occupied by the Vandals. From his pen are securely attested several short catechetical homilies and a work on biblical interpretation titled *The Book of Promises*. As in the case of the creed of Jerusalem (above), the creed of Carthage has been reconstructed from the bishop's address to the *competentes*, or those in the final stages of preparing for baptism.

9. Athanasian Creed (Pseudo-Athanasian Creed) (mid–5th cent.)

Whoever desires to be saved must above all things hold the catholic faith. Unless one keeps it in its entirety inviolate, one will assuredly perish eternally.
    Now this is the catholic faith, that we worship one God in Trinity and Trinity in unity, without either confusing the persons or dividing the substance. For the Father's person is one, the Son's another, the Holy Spirit's another; but the Godhead of the Father, the Son, and the Holy Spirit is one, their glory is equal, their majesty coeternal.

Such as the Father is, such is the Son, such also the Holy Spirit. The Father is unbegotten, the Son unbegotten, the Holy Spirit unbegotten. The Father is infinite, the Son infinite, the Holy Spirit infinite. The Father is eternal, the Son eternal, the Holy Spirit eternal. Yet there are not three eternals, but one eternal; just as there are not three unbegotten[4] or three infinites, but one unbegotten and one infinite. In the same way the Father is almighty, the Son almighty, the Holy Spirit almighty; yet there are not three almighties, but one Almighty.

Thus the Father is God, the Son is God, the Holy Spirit is God; and yet there are not three gods, but there is one God. Thus the Father is Lord, the Son Lord, the Holy Spirit Lord; and yet there are not three lords, but there is one Lord. Because just as we are obliged by Christian truth to acknowledge each person separately as both God and Lord, so we are forbidden by the catholic religion to speak of three gods or lords.

The Father is from none, not made nor created nor begotten. The Son is from the Father alone, not made nor created but begotten. The Holy Spirit is from the Father and the Son, not made nor created nor begotten but proceeding. So there is one Father, not three Fathers; one Son, not three Sons; one Holy Spirit, not three Holy Spirits. And in this Trinity there is nothing before or after, nothing greater or less, but all three persons are coeternal with each other and coequal. Thus in all things, as has been stated above, both Trinity in unity and unity in Trinity must be worshiped. So the one who desires to be saved should think of the Trinity in this way.

It is necessary, however, to eternal salvation that one should also faithfully believe in the incarnation of our Lord Jesus Christ. Now the right faith is that we should believe and confess that our Lord Jesus Christ, the Son of God, is equally both God and man.

He is God from the Father's substance, begotten before time; and he is man from his mother's substance, born in time. Perfect God, perfect man composed of a rational soul and human flesh, equal to the Father in respect of his divinity, less than the Father in respect of his humanity.

Who, although he is God and man, is nevertheless not two but one Christ. He is one, however, not by the transformation of his divinity into flesh, but by the taking up of his humanity into God; one certainly not by confusion of substance, but by oneness of

4. *Tres increati.*

person. For just as rational soul and flesh are a single man, so God and man are a single Christ.

Who suffered for our salvation, descended into hell, rose from the dead, ascended into heaven, sat down at the Father's right hand, whence he will come to judge living and dead: at whose coming all men will rise again with their bodies, and will render an account of their deeds; and those who have lived well will go to eternal life, those who have lived badly to eternal fire.

This is the catholic faith. Unless one believes it faithfully and steadfastly, one will not be able to be saved. (J. N. D. Kelly, *The Athanasian Creed* [New York: Harper & Row, 1964], 17–20, slightly adapted)

More of a doctrinal manifesto than a creed, the so-called Athanasian Creed was not written by Athanasius, though it was attributed to him by many manuscripts until the later Middle Ages. It is commonly called the Quicunque Creed, because this is the first word of the text (Latin for "Whoever")—not an untypical practice in the medieval copying of ancient texts. Its earliest appearance is in the writings of Caesarius of Arles (bishop in 502–42), and excerpts of it are found in Vincent of Lérins (450); both occurrences suggest that its place of origin is from southern Gaul. This Western statement of faith greatly influenced confessional and theological development in medieval reformation theology.

B. Conciliar Creeds: Ecumenical (or "Great") Creeds

Unlike the church creeds above, these statements of faith are derived from the doctrinal deliberations of a council. Yet they were not completely artificial declarations foisted on churches by the bishops. General creeds of the fourth and fifth centuries were deemed authoritative by the churches who received them because they were viewed as faithful conductors of the Christian doctrine of God found in Scripture and the tradition.

1. Nicene Creed (325)

We believe in one God, the Father, almighty, maker of all things visible and invisible;

and in one Lord Jesus Christ, the Son of God, begotten from the Father, only-begotten, that is, from the substance of the Father, God from God, Light from Light, true God from true God, begotten not made, of one substance from the Father, through whom all things came into being, things in heaven and things on earth, who because of us men and because of our salvation came down and became incarnate, becoming man, suffered and rose again

on the third day, ascended to the heavens, will come to judge the
living and the dead;
   and in the Holy Spirit.

(Greek and Latin versions in Schaff,
The Creeds of Christendom, 2:60)

An anathema (a condemnation) immediately follows the creed, further elaborating the rejection of any view that characterizes the Son as not existing at any previous point, or that the begetting of the Son by the Father occurred in time, or that the Son was not eternally begotten: "But as for those who say, 'There was when he was not,' and, 'Before being born he was not,' and 'He came into existence out of nothing,' or who assert that the Son of God is a different hypostasis or substance, or is subject to change or alteration—these the catholic and apostolic church anathematizes."

The creed (originally in Greek) is first quoted in a letter written by Eusebius of Caesarea (probably in 325) to his congregation, explaining why he had subscribed to the creed instead of sticking to the church's own baptismal creed. Not surprisingly, Athanasius quotes the creed two times.[5] The first known Latin version, by Hilary of Poitiers,[6] surfaces about the same time. In the later fourth century, Greek and Latin versions of the creed rapidly multiplied. By the sixth century, it became a part of the Eastern liturgy, and soon after, the Western, though in the form of B.5, below.

2. The Nicene Creed in Prayer

We believe
in one God
Father Almighty,
Creator of all things
visible and invisible,
and in one Lord Jesus Christ
the Son of God
begotten of the Father, only-begotten,
that is, from the substance
of the Father, God from
God, Light from
Light, True God
from True God,
begotten
and not made,

---

5. In the appendix of *On the Definition of the Nicene Creed* (where he merely replicates Eusebius of Caesarea's letter) and a decade later in a letter to the emperor Jovinian.

6. *On the Synods* 84; and the first "book" of his *Against Ursacius and Valens* (both written in late 357 or 358).

of the same substance as the
Father, through whom all
things were made
which are in heaven and
on earth, who
for us men and for
our salvation,
came down,
was made flesh. . . .

(W. F. Macomber, "The Nicene Creed in a Liturgical
Fragment of the 5th or 6th Century from Upper Egypt,"
Oriens christianus 77 [1993]: 98–103)

In some Eastern churches, the Nicene Creed eventually came to function as the liturgical confession in the worship services. The earliest example of the Nicene Creed (not the Niceno-Constantinopolitan Creed) used in a church liturgy comes from two Greek fragments on parchment originally found in Egypt and dated to the late fifth or sixth century. The fragments, two contiguous sections from the midst of a longer text, measure 11.9 cm x 9.3 cm and 8.3 cm x 4.6 cm respectively (now found in Brigham Young University Collection, Coptic Fragments #90).

The citation of the creed appears at the end of a prayer, apparently offered during the celebration of the Eucharist. Arrangement and translation of the above lines follows the spacing of the fragment.

3. Teaching the Nicene Creed (ca. 370)

We believe in one God, Father Almighty, maker of things visible and invisible,

and in our one Lord, Jesus Christ, the Son of God, born of the Father, that is, from the substance of the Father, God from God, Light from Light, True God from True God, born not made, of one substance with the Father, which the Greeks call *homoousion*, through whom all things were made whether in heaven or on the earth, who for us men and for our salvation came down and was incarnate, he was made man. He suffered, he arose again on the third day; he ascended into heaven; he will come to judge the living and the dead.

And [we believe] in the Holy Spirit.

[Those who say "There was once (when) he was not," and "Before he was born he was not," and "He was made from nothing or from another substance," the Son of God is mutable and subject to change, he will suffer perpetual punishments when he is sent to

Gehenna by the command of the Father, by the command of the
Son, by the urging of the Holy Spirit.][7]
The Catholic Faith Fides as set forth at Nicaea
Amen.

(C. H. Turner, ed., *Ecclesiae occidentalis monumenta
iuris antiquissima: Canonum et conciliorum Graecorum
interpretationes Latinae* [Oxford: Clarendon, 1939],
I.2, appendix X, 330–47,
reconstructed and trans. D. H. Williams)

The above text (based on a sole manuscript from the ninth century) is reconstructed
from an anonymous Latin work composed for an unknown audience in the latter fourth
century. It reads like a commentary,[8] explaining each clause of the Nicene Creed with the
purpose of teaching Christians how properly to understand their faith in light of the creed's
truths. The overall argument of the whole text is that the truth about the Nicene creed is
found entirely in Scripture. Every chapter of the commentary contains numerous whole or
partial citations from Old and New Testaments. The writer seems to be implicitly refuting
any charge that the Nicene Creed was not biblical, a charge to which opponents of Nicaea
often appealed.

Although the text frequently attacks the "Arians," it is more of a theological catechism than
a polemical work. This text is another indication that the Nicene Creed with its doctrine was
becoming generally accepted by Western churches as a unique statement of orthodoxy after
the 350s. Western versions similar to the one above can be found in Hilary of Poitiers, Gregory
of Elvira, and several others of the same period. A shared characteristic of the Western versions
of the text is the explanation of "one substance" as "what the Greeks call *homoousion*."

4. Creed of Constantinople (381)

The Symbol of the One Hundred and Fifty at Constantinople.

We believe in one God, Father Almighty, maker of heaven and
earth, and of all things visible and invisible,

And in one Lord Jesus Christ, the unique Son of God begotten
of the Father before all the ages, Light of Light, true God of true
God, begotten, not made, of one substance with the Father, through
whom all things came into being; who for us men and for our
salvation came down from heaven, and was incarnate of the Holy
Spirit and Mary the Virgin, and became man; he was crucified also
for us under Pontius Pilate, and suffered, and was buried, and rose
again on the third day according to the Scriptures; and ascended

---

7. While not appended to the last line of the creed, the author treats the anathema as
part of the creed.

8. Which is why Turner named the text *Commentarius in Symbolum Nicaeanum.*

into heaven, and sits on the right hand of the Father, and is coming again with glory to judge living and dead; of whose Kingdom
there will be no end.

And in the Holy Spirit, the Lord, and the Life-giver, who proceeds
from the Father, who with the Father and the Son is worshiped and
glorified, who spoke through the prophets; in one Holy Catholic
and Apostolic Church; we confess one Baptism for the remission
of sins. We look for the resurrection of the dead, and the life of the
age to come. Amen. (LCC 3:372)

The text of the Constantinopolitan Creed comes from the proceedings of the Council of
Chalcedon (451), some seventy years later. Apparently no records about this creed were immediately available or widespread after the council of 381. This may have been because this
council was not really "ecumenical" since all the attendees were from the East, and because
the council was primarily about ratifying the Nicene Creed as the only acceptable creed in the
East. For whatever reason, we first hear of this creed at the time of Chalcedon.

Despite its reaffirmation of Nicaea, the Constantinopolitan Creed makes some minor changes
by omitting the Nicene phrases "God from God," and "from the substance of the Father," and
elaborating on the person of the Holy Spirit and its implications for the church. The third
ecumenical council of Ephesus (431), which did not produce a creed, likewise acknowledges
the final authority of the Nicene Creed. But because of theological subtleties produced by
unscrupulous persons intending to distort the intended meaning, "it has proved necessary
to add testimonies from the holy and orthodox fathers that can fill out the meaning" of the
words proclaimed in the creed (canon 7 of the Nicene Creed).

5. The Western Niceno-Constantinopolitan Creed (6th cent.)

We believe in one God the Father almighty, Maker of heaven and
of earth, of all that is seen and unseen;

And in one Lord Jesus Christ, the only-begotten Son of God, born
of the Father before all the ages, God from God,[9] light from light,
true God from true God, begotten not made, consubstantial with the
Father, through whom all things were made; who for us men and for
our salvation he came down from heaven. And he became incarnate
by the Holy Spirit and the virgin Mary, was made man. He also was
crucified for our sake under Pontius Pilate, suffered and was buried
and rose up on the third day in accordance with the Scriptures,
ascended into heaven, and sits on the right hand of the Father. He
will come again with glory to judge the living and the dead, and his
kingdom will have no end.

9. "God from God" is from the Nicene Creed, though it does not appear in the earlier
Greek version of the Niceno-Constantinopolitan Creed (§3).

And in the Holy Spirit, the Lord and Life-giver: who proceeds from the Father and the Son. With the Father and Son, he is likewise worshiped and glorified who has spoken through the prophets. And in one, holy, catholic, and apostolic church. We confess one baptism for the forgiveness of sins. We look forward to the resurrection of the dead and the life in the ages to come. Amen. (*Creeds and Confessions* 1:670)

This is the creed most often used in Western church liturgies today as the "Nicene Creed." The most controversial alteration in this Latin version of the Niceno-Constantinopolitan creed is the insertion of "and the Son" (*filioque*) in the third paragraph, speaking of the Spirit's procession. Because the West by this time was dominated by Augustinian trinitarian theology, the insertion may have stemmed from a desire to make the creed more compatible with a view of the complete unity of God's being and activity; that anything the Father does, so does the Son and the Spirit. If the Spirit proceeds from the Father, then the Spirit must proceed from the Son. To this day the Eastern Orthodox tradition rejects this insertion as tampering with the original creedal text and maintains that there is only one divine procession.

6. Creed of Chalcedon (451)

Following therefore the holy Fathers, we confess one and the same our Lord Jesus Christ, and we all teach harmoniously that he is the same perfect in Godhead, the same perfect in manhood, truly God and truly man, the same of a rational soul and body; consubstantial with the Father in Godhead, and the same consubstantial with us in manhood, like us in all things except sin; begotten before ages of the Father in Godhead, the same in the last days for us; and for our salvation born of Mary the virgin, the God-bearer,[10] in manhood, one and the same Christ, Son, Lord, unique; acknowledged in two natures without confusion, without change, without division, without separation, the difference of the natures being by no means taken away because of the union, but rather the distinctive character of each nature being preserved, and [each] combining in one Person and being[11]—divided or separated into two Persons, but one and the same Son and only-begotten God, Word, Lord Jesus Christ; as the prophets of old and the Lord Jesus Christ himself taught us about him, and the symbol of the fathers has handed down to us. (LCC 3:373, slightly modified)

10. *Theotokos* (lit., "God-bearer"), a term commonly used by Alexandrian bishops as a means of expressing that the full divinity of the Son was born with his full humanity from Mary.
11. *Hypostasis.*

It is apparent that what is called the Chalcedon Creed is not really a creed in the usual sense of a trinitarian formula, but a series of qualifications of the second article of the Nicene Creed. This interpretation is borne out by Chalcedon's conclusion: "Since we have determined these things with all possible accuracy and care, the holy and ecumenical Council has decreed that no one shall be allowed to bring forward another Creed, nor to compose or produce or think out or teach [such] to others." The "Creed" referenced here is the Nicene Creed, which is being sanctioned against the introduction of any other creed.

C. Conciliar Creeds: Regional

1. Antioch (325)

This, then, is the faith that was set forth by spiritual men, whom it is not right to think of as living or understanding according to the flesh at any time, but as always formed and trained in the Spirit by means of the holy writings of the inspired books.

It is: to believe in one God, the Father, the ruler of all, incomprehensible, immutable, and unchanging, the providential overseer and governor of all things, righteous and good, Maker of heaven and earth and all that is in them, Lord of the law and the prophets and the New Covenant; and in one Lord Jesus Christ, the only-begotten Son, begotten not out of nonexistence, but out of the Father, not as a thing made but as a begotten being in the strict sense, generated in an unutterable and indescribable fashion, since only the Father who begat and the Son who was begotten know—"No one knows the Father except the Son, or the Son except the Father." He always exists and did not at any earlier time not exist.[12] For we have learned from the Holy Scriptures that he is the sole image [of the Father], and is not un-begotten, since it is clear that he is, so to speak, "from" the Father. The Scriptures call him a begotten son, in the strict and proper sense—not just by convention,[13] for it would be irreverent and blasphemous to say this. Just so do we believe that he is immutable and unchanging, not begotten or brought into being by will or [only] conventionally speaking, [or?] in such a way that he would seem to be [generated] out of nonexistence,[14] but begotten in the way appropriate for him; not in the likeness or the nature of anything that has come to be

12. This sentence makes for awkward reading in any language, but the point, which was directly set against the propositions associated with Arius, was that the Son always existed with the Father and is therefore eternal as the Father is eternal.

13. That is, he is truly the Son and not the Father just using a different name.

14. The exact meaning of this sentence is unclear.

through him, or mixed with them at all—which it is not lawful to imagine. Rather do we confess, then, because he transcends all conception or understanding or thought, that he was begotten out of the unbegotten Father, God the Word, the true light, righteousness, Jesus Christ, the Lord and Savior of all. For he is the image, not of the will or anything else, but of the actual being[15] of the Father. This Son, God the Word, having also been born and made flesh out of Mary the Mother of God[16] and suffered, and died, rose from the dead and, when he had been taken into heaven, took his seat on the right hand of the power of the Most High, and is coming to judge the living and the dead.

Further, as the Holy Scriptures teach us to put our faith in our Savior, so too they teach us to put our faith in the one Spirit, the one catholic Church, the resurrection of the dead, and a judgment in which everyone will he repaid for what they have done in the flesh, whether good things or bad, and we anathematize those who say or think or preach that the Son of God is a creature or something brought into being or made and is not truly a begotten being, or that there was when he was not.[17] (Letter from the Synod of Antioch; Williams, *Arius*, 275–76)

It was not until the early twentieth century that this conciliar letter of the council was rediscovered. The letter, which exists only in Syriac translation, contains a strongly anti-Arian creedal statement. The synod condemned several theologians for subordinationism, including Eusebius of Caesarea. While gathered they also produced the earliest example of a conciliar creed, predating the Nicene formulation by several months. The condemnations and the creed, however, were only provisional measures. Bishops meeting in Antioch were already looking forward to a larger council that was slated to meet within the same year in the city of Ancyra. Location of this intended council was then moved to Nicaea, at which was produced the formula known as the Nicene Creed.

2. Creed of Antioch (341)

Following the evangelical and apostolic tradition, we believe in one God, the Ruler of all, the Former and Maker and Provider of everything, from whom are all things;

and in one Lord, Jesus Christ, his Son the only-begotten God, through whom are all things, begotten from the Father before all

---

15. *Hypostasis.*
16. *Theotokos.*
17. This anathema, or condemnation, specifically refutes the teaching of Arius as expressed in one of his letters. The Nicene Creed, issued that same year, likewise anathematized this teaching.

ages, God from God, entire fullness from entire fullness, the Only One from the Only One, the Perfect from the Perfect, King from King, Lord from Lord, the living Word, living wisdom, true light, the way, the truth, the resurrection, the shepherd, the door; immutable and unchanging, the exact image of the substance and will and power and glory of the Father's divinity, "the firstborn of all creation" [Col. 1:15], the one who is "in the beginning with God" [John 1:2], God the Word, according to what is said in the Gospel: "and the Word was God," [John 1:1], "through whom all things came to be" [John 1:3], and "in whom all things cohere" [Col. 1:17], who in the last days came down from above and was begotten of a virgin, in accordance with the Scriptures, and became a human being, "a mediator between God and human beings" [1 Tim. 2:5], the apostle of our faith and author of life, as he says: "I have come down from heaven not to do my own will, but the will of him who sent me" [John 6:38]: who suffered on our behalf and rose on the third day and ascended into the heavens, and took his seat on the Father's right hand, and is coming again with glory and power to judge living and dead;

and in the Holy Spirit, given to believers for encouragement and sanctification and perfection, just as our Lord Jesus Christ ordered his disciples: "Go forth and teach all nations, baptizing them in the name of the Father and of the Son and of the Holy Spirit" [Matt. 28:19]—that is, of a Father who truly is Father, a Son who truly is Son, a Holy Spirit who truly is Holy Spirit—these names are not assigned casually or idly, but designate quite precisely the particular subsistence,[18] the rank, and the glory of each of those named, so as to make them three in respect of subsistence, but one in concord. (Athanasius, *On the Synods* 23; *Creeds and Confessions*, 89)

Of the four creeds associated with the council of Antioch of 341 (also known as the Dedication Council), only the so-called "second creed" was issued by the council in its own name. A church baptismal creed is the basis for this statement, possibly the creed used in the Antiochene church. Its long and rambling wording is due to biblical and theological qualifications made at various points.

The Antiochene Creed is purposely offering a confessional alternative to the views expressed at Nicaea (325). It is not a pro-Arian statement of faith, even though it supports a hierarchical trinitarianism. Three separate hypostases of the Father, the Son, and the Spirit are indeed ranked in a manner reminiscent of third-century theology. This position, however, was also standard fare against Monarchianism, which was closely associated with Marcellus of Ancyrus, who had been one of the leading architects of the Nicene Creed. Because Nicaea

18. "Subsistence" is used here and later in the sentence for the Greek term *hypostasis*.

had professed the Father and Son as *homoousios* (the same substance), Eastern bishops had continuing concerns that this language revealed a unitarian view of God.

3. Western Creed of Serdica (Sophia) (342–343)

But this is what we have ourselves received and been taught, this is what we hold as the catholic and apostolic tradition and faith and confession: There is one essence,[19] which the heretics themselves call "substance"[20] of the Father, the Son, and the Holy Spirit.

And if anyone should inquire, what is the substance of the Son, we confess that it is the same as that which is confessed as the Father's alone; and neither has Father ever existed without Son, nor Son without Father, nor could he be what he is, Logos-Spirit. It is quite absurd to say that the Father ever did not exist. That Father without Son can neither be named nor exist, is the Son's own testimony: "I am in the Father and the Father in me," and, "I and the Father are one." None of us denies "begotten," but begotten for things, to wit those things which are known as invisible and visible things, begotten as artificer of archangels and angels and the world, and for mankind, because it says, "Wisdom the artificer of all has taught me," and, "All things were made by him." For he could not exist forever if he had got a beginning of existence, because the Logos-God who always exists has no beginning, and is never subject to an end. We do not say that the Father is Son, nor again that the Son is Father; but the Father is Father, and the Son is the Father's Son. We confess that the Son is the Father's Power.

We confess that the Logos of God is the Father's, and beside him there is no other, and that the Logos is true God and Wisdom and Power. A true Son is part of our tradition, but we do not say that he is Son as the rest are called sons; for it is by adoption, or because of being reborn, or because they are deemed worthy that they are called sons, not because of the one substance which belongs to Father and Son.

We confess both an Only-begotten and a Firstborn; but that the Logos is only-begotten, who always was and is in the Father. "Firstborn" refers to the man, but it applies to the new creation, since he is "Firstborn from the dead."

We confess that God is One; we confess one divinity of Father and Son. And no one ever denies that the Father is greater than the

19. *Hypostasis.*
20. *Ousia.*

Son, not because of another substance, not because of difference, but because the very name itself of the Father is greater than that of the Son.

We believe and receive the Paraclete, the Holy Spirit, which the Lord himself both promised and sent to us. He it was, we believe, that was sent; and it was not he that suffered, but the man whom he put on, whom he took from Mary the Virgin, the man who was able to suffer. For a man is mortal, but God is immortal. We believe that he rose the third day; not God in the man, but the man in God arose; and he also presented him whom he had liberated as a gift to his own Father. And we believe that at a propitious and appointed time he will himself judge all men about everything. (Theodoret, *HE* 2.8.38–43; *CCC* 13–14)

4. *Creed of Ariminum (Rimini) (359)*

We believe in one God, Father Almighty, from whom are all things [Rom. 11:36],

And in the unique Son of God, who was begotten of God before all ages and before all beginning, through whom all things came into being, both visible and invisible, begotten uniquely, only from the Father only, God of God, like to the Father who begot him, according to the Scriptures, whose generation no one knows [Isa. 53:8] except only the Father who begot him. We know that this unique Son of God came from heaven, the Father sending him, as it is written, for the destruction of sin and death, and was born of the Holy Spirit, of Mary the Virgin according to the flesh, as it is written, and companied with the disciples, and when all the dispensation was fulfilled according to the Father's will, was crucified and died and was buried and descended into the lower regions, before whom hell itself trembled [Job 38:17],[21] who also rose again from the dead on the third day and dwelt among the disciples, and when forty days were fulfilled was taken up into heaven, and sits on the right hand of the Father, [and] is to come on the last day, of the resurrection, in the Father's glory, to render to each according to his works;

And in the Holy Spirit, whom the unique Son of God himself, Christ our Lord and God, promised to send to the race of men as a Paraclete, as it is written, "the Spirit of truth" [John 14:16–17], whom he sent to them when he had ascended into heaven. But as

---

21. One of the earliest references to Christ's "harrowing of hell" (cf. 1 Pet. 3:19; 4:6).

to the word "essence,"[22] which was used by the Fathers in simplicity, but, being unknown to the people caused scandal, because the Scriptures do not contain it, it seems best that it should be taken away and no mention made of it in the future, since the divine Scriptures nowhere made mention of the essence of Father and Son; nor, similarly, should the word *hypostasis*[23] be used of Father and Son and Holy Spirit. But we say that the Son is like the Father, as the divine Scriptures say and teach; and let all heresies which have been condemned before and such recent ones as may have arisen and are contrary to this statement be anathema. (Socrates, *HE* 2.41; Theodoret, *HE* 2.18; LCC 3:342)

Though regarded heretical for its rank subordination of the Son and the Spirit to the Father, this statement of faith was embraced by the emperor Constantius II and accepted as the church's universal creed for a brief period, having been ratified at a council in Constantinople (360). It was a blatant rejection of the Nicene or any previous creed that referred to the Father and Son as having a shared "substance" or "essence." All such terminology is condemned as unscriptural. At most, the Son was said to be "like" (*homoios*) the Father. More than any other formula, the severity of the theological objections laid down in the Ariminum Creed brought about a reaction and the renewal of the Nicene faith. Nevertheless, for the next twenty years the creed issued at Ariminum, a council attended by some four hundred bishops (almost double the number of those who attended Nicaea), challenged the hegemony of the Nicene Creed. Die-hard opponents of Nicaea continued to recognize the authority of Ariminum as late as the mid-fifth century.

5. From the Council of Alexandria (362)

The following brief and clear statements are for every Christian, so that they may preserve the truth that has been preached from the beginning and upon which we stand fast and wait for the eternal hopes.

Now the mark of our faith is this: the Trinity is the same substance, and true God became human from Mary. The one who does not affirm these things let him be accursed. For the great council that was in Nicaea resolved these statements: the Son is the same substance with the Father; the Spirit is to be glorified with the Father and the Son; and true God as the Son of God became flesh, suffered, was resurrected, ascended into heaven, and will come as judge of the living and the dead. To whom the glory is forever. Amen. (*PG* 28:81–84B; trans. Derek Dodson, Baylor University)

22. *Ousia.*
23. Another word for "essence" or "substance."

Our knowledge about this Alexandrian synod, which met in the middle of 362, is founded solely upon two documents: a text transmitted under the title of *Epistola catholica*, which had been consigned to the dubious writings of the Athanasian corpus since the fifteenth century and thought to be a genuine fragment from the opening of the synodical letter produced by that assembly; and another letter from the synod known as the *Tomus ad Antiochenos* (*Treatise to the Antiochenes*). In no uncertain terms the *Epistola* set forth that the Trinity is "the same substance" (*homoousios*) as established by the Council of Nicaea (325). But the Council of Alexandria, composed of Eastern and Western bishops, agreed that the terms "substance" (*ousia*), which the Westerners favored, and "essence" (*hypostasis*), which most Easterners favored, were both legitimate for describing God's being. This decision opened the way for the eventual solidarity between East and West about understanding the Nicene faith.

INTERPRETING THE BIBLE

A. Peter's First Sermon: Hebrew Scripture Tells of the Apostolic Message

Men of Israel, listen to this: Jesus of Nazareth was a man accredited by God to you by miracles, wonders and signs, which God did among you through him, as you yourselves know. This man was handed over to you by God's set purpose and foreknowledge; and you, with the help of wicked men, put him to death by nailing him to the cross. But God raised him from the dead, freeing him from the agony of death, because it was impossible for death to keep its hold on him. David said this about him:

> "I saw the Lord always before me.
>   Because he is at my right hand,
>   I will not be shaken.
> Therefore my heart is glad and my tongue rejoices;
>   my body also will live in hope,
> because you will not abandon me to the grave,
>   nor will you let your Holy One see decay.
> You have made known to me the paths of life;
>   you will fill me with joy in your presence."[1]

1. Ps. 16:8–11. It was assumed by Jewish and Christian writers that David wrote all the Psalms.

Brothers, I can tell you confidently that the patriarch David died and was buried, and his tomb is here to this day.[2] But he was a prophet and knew that God had promised him on oath that he would place one of his descendents on his throne [2 Sam. 7:12]. Seeing what was ahead, he spoke of the resurrection of the Christ,[3] that he was not abandoned to the grave, nor did his body see decay. God has raised this Jesus to life, and we are all witnesses of the fact. Exalted to the right hand of God,[4] he has received from the Father the promised Holy Spirit[5] and has poured out what you now see and hear. For David did not ascend to heaven, and yet he said,

> "The Lord said to my Lord:
>   'Sit at my right hand
> until I make your enemies
>   a footstool for your feet.'"[6] (Acts 2:22–35)

This first sermon of Peter after the resurrection and ascension of Christ furnishes the basic content of the tradition (or, in this case, the apostolic preaching), which was already being formed and which we find in the writings of other apostles and beyond. Among the basic propositions in this presentation is that followers of Jesus have a connected history with Israel and the promises of the Hebrew Scriptures; that God raised Jesus from the dead and exalted him, which demonstrates that Jesus is the fulfiller of God's covenant; that with repentance, forgiveness of sins comes through the name of Jesus the Christ; and that the gift of the Holy Spirit is bestowed on the new believer.

B. Tertullian: Paul and Rule (ca. 200)

Of the apostles, John and Matthew were the first to instill the faith into us, whereas the apostolic men,[7] Luke and Mark, reaffirm it afterward. These all start with the same principles of the Rule, as it relates to the one and only God the creator and his Christ, how

2. The implication is that the psalm's content could not have been referring to David.

3. "Christ" is the Greek word for the Hebrew term "Messiah."

4. Compare Paul's Philippian "hymn" (Phil. 2:8b–9a): "He became obedient to death— even death on a cross. Therefore God has exalted him to the highest place."

5. For the pattern of language that describes the divine plan in terms of God the Father, Christ the Son, and the Holy Spirit, see also 2 Cor. 13:14; Matt. 28:19.

6. Ps. 110:1. Cf. Phil. 2:10: "that at the name of Jesus every knee should bow, in heaven and on earth and under the earth."

7. Lit., *apostolicos*, companions of the apostles (Mark of Peter, Luke of Paul)

he was born of the Virgin, and came to fulfill the Law and the Prophets. Never mind if there occurs some variation in the order of the narratives, as long as there is agreement in the essential things of the faith. . . .

Let us see what milk the Corinthians drank from Paul; to what Rule (of Faith) the Galatians were brought for correction; what the Philippians, the Thessalonians, the Ephesians read by it; what utterance also the Romans give. (*Against Marcion* 4.2, 5; *ANF* 3:347, 350, modified)

The tradition in the form of the Rule of Faith was not a novel set of practices made as an addition to Scripture. It was not from outside the faith. On the contrary, Tertullian claimed that the tradition had been kept "as a sacred deposit in the churches of the apostles" (*Against Marcion* 4.5).

C. Melito of Sardis: From Shadow to the Reality (late 2nd cent.)

A preliminary sketch is made of a future thing
    out of wax or of clay or of wood,
    in order that what will soon arise
taller in height,
    stronger in power,
    beautiful in form,
    rich in its construction,
may be seen through a small and perishable sketch.
But when that of which it is the model arises,
    that which once bore the image of the future thing
    is itself destroyed as growing useless
    having yielded to what is truly real the image of it;
    and what once was precious becomes worthless
    when what is truly precious has been revealed.
The people then was a model by way of preliminary sketch,
    and the law was the writing of a parable;
    the Gospel is the recounting and fulfillment of the law,
    and the Church is the repository of the reality.
The model then was precious before the reality,
    and the parable was marvelous before the interpretation;
    that is, the people were precious before the Church arose,
    and the law was marvelous before the Gospel was
        elucidated.
But when the Church arose

and the Gospel took precedence,
    the model was made void, conceding its power to the
        reality,
    and the law was fulfilled, conceding its power to the
        Gospel.

> (Stuart George Hall, ed., *On Pascha and Fragments: Melito
> of Sardis*, Oxford Early Christian Texts [Oxford: Clarendon,
> 1979])

Little is known about Melito, bishop of Sardis, in western Asia Minor (today's Turkey), with the exception of some fragments from other works (see chap. 9.B, below) and this sermon on the Passover, which was not discovered until 1932. It was apparently delivered in a worship service after the reading of Exodus 12:11–30. While it is likely that the sermon was given during Eastertide, it is clear that Melito intended to tell the salvation story, moving from God's promises and works under the old covenant to the gospel of Christ and the rise of the church. In the telling of the story in verse style, we see how early Christian exegesis united both Testaments in the course of declaring its message.

D. Hippolytus of Rome: How the Right Use of Scripture Leads to Right Relation between Doctrine and Scripture (ca. 215)

Some others are secretly introducing another doctrine, who have become disciples of one Noetus, who was a native of Smyrna, (and) lived not very long ago. This person was greatly puffed up and inflated with pride, being inspired by the conceit of a strange spirit. He alleged that Christ was the Father himself, and that the Father himself was born, and suffered, and died.[8]

Then the blessed elders called him again before them and examined him. But he opposed them, saying, "What evil, then, am I doing in glorifying Christ?" And the elders replied to him, "We too know in truth one God; we know also Christ; we know that the Son suffered even as he suffered, and died even as he died, and rose again on the third day, and is at the right hand of the Father, and is coming to judge the living and the dead. These things which we have learned, so we declare."[9]

---

8. This view, known as modalism, was a unitarianism that emphasized the identity of the Father, Son, and Holy Spirit to the point of abrogating substantial distinctions of the three.

9. The elders are citing their commitment to the church's baptismal faith.

Now they seek to exhibit the foundation for their teaching by citing the verses in the law, "I am the God of your fathers: ye shall have no other gods beside me" [Exod. 20:2–3]; and again in another passage, "I am the first," he said, "and the last; and beside me there is none other" [Isa. 44:6]. Thus they say that they prove God is one. And then they reply [when questioned by the elders], "When I acknowledge Christ to be God, he is therefore the Father himself, if he is indeed God; and Christ suffered, being himself God; and consequently the Father suffered, for he was the Father himself."

But his case does not stand, for the Scriptures do not set forth the matter in this way. He chooses to promote these teachings, . . . making use only of one class of passages, . . . but he cites the words without understanding what precedes them. Yet whenever he wishes to attempt anything underhanded, he mutilates the Scriptures. But let him quote the passage as a whole, and he will discover the reason why it was written in the first place.

The Father decrees, the Word executes, and the Son is manifested, through whom the Father is believed. The economy of harmony[10] is led back to one God; for God is One. It is the Father who commands, and the Son who obeys, and the Holy Spirit who gives understanding: the Father who is above all, and the Son who is through all, and the Holy Spirit who is in all. And we cannot otherwise think of one God, but by believing in truth in Father and Son and Holy Spirit.

The whole of the Scriptures, then, proclaim this truth. (*Against Noetus* 1–3; *ANF* 5:223–24, significantly modified)

The extract is from a polemical work, originally in Greek and written by Hippolytus against a widespread doctrinal position: that the Bible proves there is one and only one God, which means that the Trinity is merely three names for the one God or three different modes of the one God in history. Modern scholars refer to this view as Modalist Monarchianism,[11] a perspective that was strongly opposed to polytheism and did not want Christianity to be considered a religion that worshipped three Gods. What lay at the heart of Hippolytus's remarks is how Scripture should be properly interpreted since the Monarchians use the same Scripture. The problem is that they use only select passages, not looking at the Bible as a whole, and that they do not regard the church's tradition, which also enables the right interpretation.

10. The term "economy" ("dispensation" in Latin), used earlier by Tertullian, signified the different functions within the Trinity, thus distinguishing them from one another.
11. Known by the ancients as patripassianism (the suffering Father).

E. Origen

1. God's Music (ca. 250)

When a person acquainted with the music of God appears, one who is wise both in words and deeds [Luke 7:22], . . . then this person will produce the sound of the music of God, since he has learned from all this how to strike the chords at the appropriate time: now the chords of the Law, now the chords of the Gospels in harmony with them, and now the chords of the Prophets. And when what is reasonable demands it, he strikes also the Apostolic chords with them, and so also the Apostolic chords with the Gospels. For this person recognizes that all of Scripture is the one perfect and harmonious instrument of God, which raises a single saving voice from the various different sounds for the benefit of everyone who desires to learn. (fragment 2 from the *Commentary on Matthew* as preserved in the *Philocalia* 6; *ANF* 9:413, adapted)

2. Knock, Seek, Ask

Always study the divine scriptures. Study them I say. For we require the deep study of the divine writings, lest we should speak of them faster than we think; and while you study these divine works with a believing and God-pleasing intention, knock at that [door] which is closed in them, and it shall be opened to you. . . .

While you attend to this divine reading correctly and with an unwavering faith in God, seek the hidden sense, which is present in most passages of the divine Scriptures. And do not be content with knocking and seeking, for what is most necessary for understanding divine things is prayer. In urging us to this the Savior says not only, "Knock and it shall be opened to you," and "Seek and you shall find," but also, "Ask, and it shall be given you" [Matt. 7:7–8]. (Origen's Letter to Gregory Thaumaturgos 3; *ANF* 4:394, adapted)

Gregory of Neocaesarea (ca. 340), also known as the Wonderworker (Thaumaturgos), was a pupil and close friend of Origen's in Alexandria. Besides his admiration for Origen's genius, Gregory learned from him principles of biblical interpretation. So high was his estimation of his former teacher that Gregory wrote an address and panegyric of Origen, praising the latter's skills along with the virtues of the Christian life and faith.

3. How Scripture Should Be Interpreted (ca. 225)

Now that we have spoken cursorily about the inspiration of the divine scriptures it is necessary to discuss the manner in which they are to be read and understood, since many mistakes have been made in consequence of the method by which the holy documents ought to be interpreted not having been discovered by the multitude. For the hard-hearted and ignorant members of the circumcision have refused to believe in our Savior because they think that they are keeping closely to the language of the prophecies that relate to him, and they see that he did not literally "proclaim release to captives" [Isa. 61:1] or build what they consider to be a real "city of God" [Ps. 46:4], or "cut off the chariots from Ephraim and the horse from Jerusalem" [Zech. 9:10], or "eat butter and honey, and choose the good before he knew or preferred the evil" [Isa. 7:15]. . . .

Ignorant assertions about God appear to be nothing else but this: that scripture is not understood in its spiritual sense, but is interpreted according to the bare letter.[12] On this account we must explain to those who believe that the sacred books are not the works of men, but that they were composed and have come down to us as a result of the inspiration of the Holy Spirit by the will of the Father of the universe through Jesus Christ, what are the methods of interpretation that appear right to us, who keep to the rule of the heavenly Church of Jesus Christ through the succession from the Apostles. . . .

. . . We ought to portray the meaning of the sacred writings in a threefold way upon one's own soul, so that the simple person may be edified by what we may call the body of the scriptures (for such is the name we may give to the common and literal interpretation); while those who have begun to make a little progress and are able to perceive something more than that may be edified by the soul of scripture; and those who are perfect and like those whom the apostle says: "We speak wisdom among the perfect; yet a wisdom not of this world, nor of the rulers of this world, which are coming to nothing; but we speak God's wisdom hidden in a mystery, the wisdom which God foreordained before the worlds unto our glory"—such as these may be edified by that spiritual law, which has "a shadow of the good things to come," as if by the Spirit. Just as man, therefore, is said to consist of body, soul and spirit, so also does the holy scripture, which has been bestowed by the

---

12. To assert that Scripture should be read only according to the literal sense was to deny the divine inspiration of the Bible.

divine bounty for man's salvation. (*On First Principles* 4.2.1–2, 4; Butterworth, *Origen*, 269–76)

The patristic approach to biblical interpretation could be unpredictable at times, but it was circumscribed by an entire theological vision (summarized in the Rule or creed). Various approaches to discovering meanings or senses thought to be inherent to Scripture partly formed the basis of this vision. Then the vision made it possible to discern relationships between God and history, Christ and church, and theology and spirituality. These senses varied among ancient writers between three (literal, moral, and mystical or spiritual) or four (literal, moral, anagogical, and allegorical),[13] but the basic idea was the same: God had "built" these possible interpretations into the text for the edification and perfecting of his people.

F. Athanasius: Scripture as the Symphony of the Spirit (early 4th cent.)

Many references to the Savior are given special prominence in every one of the books of the Scriptures, and what is proclaimed is the one and same symphony of the Spirit. . . . The same Spirit is over all, and each book ministers and fulfills the grace given to it according to what is apportioned to each by the Spirit, whether it be prophecy, lawmaking, recording of history, or the grace of the Psalms. It is one and the same Spirit to whom all these diverse gifts belong, and yet who is indivisible by nature. So while the disclosures are in accord with the variety of gifts of the Spirit in relation to the ministry that each book enjoys, the whole Spirit is in each book.

Let then the grace of the Spirit be common to all the Scriptures; let it be found in each book individually, and yet the same grace for all, just as the need demands and the Spirit wills. The distribution of the gifts does not reflect that one need is greater or lesser than another. What matters is that each fulfills and perfects one's own particular ministry with utmost faithfulness. (*On the Interpretation of the Psalms* 9–10; Kannengiesser, *Early Christian Spirituality*, 60–61, slightly adapted)

Oddly enough, Athanasius never produced a biblical commentary in his forty-five years of ministry in Alexandria. By his time (bishop in 328–73), commentaries on Scripture were becoming a popular genre of teaching the Christian faith. *The Interpretation of the Psalms* is a

13. There was no uniform approach in the ancient or medieval period whether East or West; Origen, Ambrose, and Jerome follow a tripartite division, whereas a quadripartite delineation is exemplified by Clement of Alexandria, Augustine, and John Cassian. These divisions were not "airtight." Often there was overlap between meanings or their application.

personal letter that Athanasius wrote to a friend, Marcellinus. It is not surprising that Athanasius should receive a request about understanding the Psalms, since these functioned as the church's primary hymnbook.

G. Cyril of Jerusalem: The One Spirit of the Old and New Testaments (ca. 350)

Let no one draw a line between the Old Testament and the New. Let no one say that the Spirit in the Old Testament is not identical with the Spirit of the New. For whosoever does this offends none other than the Holy Spirit who is honored with the one honor together with the Father and the Son. And it is none other than the Holy Spirit whom we receive at the moment of baptism in the three-fold name, and by its means. For the Only-begotten Son of God commanded the apostles explicitly, "Go and teach all nations, baptizing them in the name of the Father, the Son and the Holy Spirit" [Matt. 28:19]. In the Father, the Son and the Holy Spirit is our hope. We are not preaching three Gods, so let the Marcionites hold their peace. But aided by the Holy Spirit, through the one Son, we preach one God. (*Catechetical Lectures* 16.4; LCC 4:169)

Marcionite theology understood God in a manner following their sharp division of Jewish history and Christianity. The Old Testament and its law were the works of a just but harsh God, whereas Christ and the gospel were derived from the God of grace and goodness, the God of Christianity. It may be that Marcionites were accusing mainstream Christians of preaching three Gods instead of properly emphasizing only two. Cyril's point is that as the Christians teach one God as Father, Son, and Spirit, so there is one Scripture of both Testaments.

Cyril's remark should not be taken lightly. Marcionism had spread to Jerusalem, and in the same work Cyril anxiously warns new Christians not to walk into a Marcionite gathering by mistake and be taught error as truth.

H. Gregory of Nyssa: Principles for Interpreting Genesis (379–89)

According to divine inspiration with regard to the world's creation, about which the great Moses had philosophized, what on the surface seem as mere letters and as contradictory, you have enjoined us to study its development in order to understand its progression as well as to show how Holy Scripture is in agreement. . . .

With God's help we can fathom what the text means which follows a certain defined order regarding creation. "In the beginning God created the heavens and the earth" [Gen. 1:1], and the rest which pertains to the cosmogenesis[14] which the six days encompass. I think that an exposition of the words should concur with the text because God's will must conform with his divine nature, for truly his will is wisdom. . . .

"And God said, 'Let there be light'" [Gen. 1:3]. In my opinion this statement teaches that the divine word is operative in every human deliberation. We, however, consider only what has been generated and express wonder through our senses. Where fire is suddenly generated through the striking of stones or through anything which has been rendered, it exceeds the power which comprehended it and consumes the air with flames, something which we cannot fully understand.

But we claim that God's word alone is responsible for this marvel, [God] who effected it by the unutterable word of power, that is, generating light from fire. As Moses testifies in his own words, "And God said, 'Let there be light and there was light,' and God saw that it was good" [Gen. 1:3–4]. Indeed, we must behold God alone, the source of all good things. Our nature is frail, which perceives what is generated; we are unable to perceive the word by which they came into existence nor do we have the power to honor it. Praise pertains to what is known, not [to] what we do not know. (*Hexaemeron*; *PG* 44:61, 68–69, 76)

The text overall was a task of postmortem completion. Though the title of this book on the creation usually falls under Gregory's name, in actuality he finished a work already begun by his brother, Basil of Caesarea. While Gregory's intent was not to engage in the same sort of allegorizing that Origen had done, he nevertheless does not reject allegorical interpretation as Basil had done and often uses spiritual exegesis. The reason for this had to do with Gregory's firm conviction (as in the above passage) that every word of the biblical text was generated by God, though our frail natures cannot fathom God. The meaning, therefore, will be found in words and phrases, literally and spiritually.

I. Augustine

1. The Summation of the Bible's Teaching (399–400)

The narration[15] is full when each person is catechized in the first instance from what is written in the text, "In the beginning God created the heaven and the earth," on to the present times of the

14. The beginning of the world.
15. The story of the Christian Gospel.

Church. This does not imply, however, either that we ought to repeat by memory the entire Pentateuch, and the entire Books of Judges, and Kings, and Esdras,[16] and the entire Gospel and Acts of the Apostles, if we have learned all these word for word; or that we should put all the matters which are contained in these volumes into our own words, and in that manner unfold and expound them as a whole. For neither does the time admit of that, nor does any necessity demand it. . . . But what we ought to do is, to give a comprehensive statement of all things, summarily and generally, so that certain of the more wonderful facts may be selected which are listened to with superior gratification, and which have been ranked so remarkably among the exact turning-points of the history. (*On Catechizing the Uninstructed* 3.5; *NPNF* 1/3:285)

Typically, the most common context for providing an explanation of the basic message of Scripture and the creed was in catechesis or oral instruction for candidates preparing for baptism. "To catechize" in Greek means to instruct by word of mouth, and a catechumen is one who is receiving instruction from a teacher. The writing of what we call "theology" (the ancients did not use that term) was undertaken for several reasons, most of which had to do with understanding the Bible and clarifying how the Bible should be understood in the light of the church's professed faith. Thus, in teaching converts, theology was perceived as an essential element of the Christian life.

2. Love of God and Neighbor Is the Key Principle (399–400)

It is clear that on those two commandments of love to God and love to our neighbor hang not only all the law and the prophets, which at the time when the Lord spoke to that effect [Matt. 22:37–40] were as yet the only Holy Scripture,[17] but also all those books of the divine literature which have been written at a later period for our health,[18] and devoted to our remembrance. Wherefore, in the Old Testament there is a veiling of the New, and in the New Testament there is a revealing of the Old. According to that veiling, carnal men, understanding things in a carnal fashion, have been under the dominion, both then and now, of a penal fear.[19] On the other hand, spiritual men . . . have a spiritual understanding and have been made free through the love with which they have been gifted. (*On Catechizing the Uninstructed* 4.8; *NPNF* 1/3:287)

16. Ezra.
17. The Old Testament.
18. The New Testament.
19. Those who live by the law.

So if anyone who thinks that he has understood the divine scriptures or any part of them, but cannot by his understanding build
up this double love of God and neighbor, has not yet succeeded
in understanding them. (*On Christian Teaching* 1.36.40; Green, *De
doctrina christiana*, 49)

The early church did not distinguish the intellectual and practical spheres as separate do-
mains; instead, the transformation of the believer through Scripture was a moral and mental
exercise. So Augustine states, "When the person who is hearing us, or rather, who is hearing
God by us, has begun to make some progress in moral qualities and in knowledge, [he] enters
upon the way of Christ with ardor" (*On Catechizing the Uninstructed* 6.11).

3. Faith, Hope, and Love (396–426)

And so persons supported by faith, hope, and love and who keep
a firm grip on these, have no need of the Scriptures except for instructing others. That is why there are so many who live on these
three things, even in the desert without books.[20] This leads me to
think that they are a fulfillment of the saying, "If there are prophecies, they will lose their meaning; if there are tongues, they will
cease; if there is knowledge that too will lose its meaning'" [1 Cor.
13:8]. But with them, like a kind of scaffolding, such an impres-
sive structure of faith, hope, and love has been built in them so
that they do not seek what is "in part" [1 Cor. 13:9–10], for they
hold what is perfect—perfect, that is, as far as anything can be in
this life. . . .
    So when you come to realize that the "end of the law is love
from a pure heart and a good conscience and genuine faith" [1 Tim.
1:5], you will be ready to relate every interpretation of the divine
Scriptures to these three things and so be able to approach the
study of those [scriptural] books without concern. (*On Christian
Teaching* 1.39.43; 1.40.44; *WSA* 1/11:125, adapted)

For Augustine, the procedures for interpreting Scripture historically, grammatically, and
in other ways, were all secondary to the theological principles as outlined in sections G and
H, above. Understanding the Bible was impossible without having a basic grasp on Christian
moral and doctrinal standards proclaimed in the church. Such an approach meant that a

---

20. Augustine is probably thinking of the great hermit Antony, who was thought to
be illiterate and achieved a state of holiness and piety through the exercise of the Christian virtues rather then by study of holy texts. While Augustine always admired this accomplishment, he knew it was not the norm and could only serve as an inspiration for
himself and most Christians.

proper interpretation of the Bible could not be found outside the church.[21] It also prevented any individual who possessed mere knowledge of Scripture from becoming regarded as a reliable teacher of the text.

J. Diodore of Tarsus: Allegory to Be Kept in Perspective (ca. 378)

In any approach to Holy Scripture, the literal reading of the text reveals some truths while the discovery of other truths requires the application of *theōria*.[22] Given the great difference between *historia* and *theōria*, allegory and figuration[23] or parable, the interpreter must classify and determine each figurative expression with care and precision so that the reader can see what is history and what is *theōria*, and draw one's conclusions accordingly.

One must especially keep in mind the point which I have stated very clearly in my prologue to the Psalter: Holy Scripture knows the term "allegory" but not its application. Even the blessed Paul uses the term, "This is said by way of allegory, for they are two covenants" [Gal. 4:24]. But his use of the word and his application are different from the Greeks. For the Greeks speak of allegory when something is understood in one way but said in another way.[24]

But Scripture does not speak of allegory in this way. How then does it speak? Let me explain briefly. Scripture does not in any way repudiate the underlying prior history [of the text], but "theorizes," that is, it develops a higher vision (*theōria*) of other but similar events in addition, without abrogating history. . . .

Based on the historical account of Isaac and Ishmael and their mothers, Sarah and Hagar, Paul develops the higher *theōria* by understanding Hagar as Mount Sinai but Isaac's mother as the free Jerusalem, the future mother of all believers. (Preface to the *Commentary on Psalm 118*; Froehlich, *Biblical Interpretation*, 87–88, modified)

In reaction to perceived extremes in allegorical exegesis practiced in Alexandria and elsewhere, Diodore, along with his former pupils, Theodore of Mopsuestia and John Chrysostom,

21. The patristic era took seriously the scriptural dictum that the interpretation of Scripture is not a matter of "the prophet's own interpretation" (2 Pet. 1:20).

22. Lit., a perception of mind or spirit, often translated as "contemplation."

23. Lit., *tropologia*.

24. Diodore offers several examples from Greek literature. Zeus's intercourse with Hera, which leads to offspring, is allegorized to mean that when ether, a fiery element, is mixed with air, it influences the affairs of humanity on earth.

sought a more balanced approach to biblical interpretation. But in no sense is history being set against or preferred to *theōria*; in fact, the higher vision was the rightful culmination of the *historia*. Furthermore, *theōria* was not so far apart from what many meant by allegory: leading the reader upward into spiritual truths that are not obvious in the text, thus providing a fuller understanding of God's salvific plan. In this sense, then, *theōria* for Diodore was much like what other patristic writers called anagogy.

K. Augustine: Literal or Allegorical Interpretation? (396–426)

First of all, we must point out the method for discovering if an expression is proper or figurative. And here, quite simply, is the one and only method: anything in the divine writings that cannot be referred either to good, honest morals or to the truth of faith, you must know is said figuratively. Good honest morals belong to loving God and one's neighbor; the truth of the faith belongs to knowing God and one's neighbor. As for hope, that lies in each person's own conscience,[25] to the extent that you perceive yourself to be making progress in the love of God and neighbor, and in the knowledge of them. . . .

Any harsh and even cruel word or deed attributed to God or his saints that is found in the holy Scriptures has to do with the destruction of the human kingdom of wrong desires. If the word or deed is clear, it should not be treated as figurative and related to something else. For example, Paul's saying, "You are storing up wrath for yourself on the day of wrath, the day of the revelation of the just judgment of God." . . . But this was written to those whose destruction must accompany their wrong desires; they who refused to control them. . . .[26]

If the [biblical] expression is a prescriptive one, and either forbids wickedness or wrongdoing, or endorses self-interest or kindness, it is not figurative. But if a passage seems to endorse wickedness or wrongdoing or to forbid selflessness or kindness, it is figurative.[27]

25. A reference to 1 Tim. 1:5, where love and faith are mentioned, and hope is found in the guise of a good conscience.

26. Augustine cites here Rom. 2:5–9 and argues that the words ought to be taken literally since they speak of God bringing deserved destruction for the reasons of judgment.

27. Evil words or deeds reported to be spoken or done by God or those doing his will (especially as it concerns the Old Testament) should not be taken literally. Such words or deeds are indicative of a deeper meaning of the text that the reader must investigate since God is good and since the purpose of Scripture is to engender our love for him and for our neighbor.

Scripture says, "Unless you eat the flesh of the Son of man and drink his blood, you will not have life within you" [John 6:53]. This seems to endorse wickedness or wrongdoing, and so it is figurative: a command to participate in the Lord's passion and to keep in our memory grateful and useful knowledge that his flesh was crucified and wounded for our sake.

Scripture says, "If your enemy is hungry, feed him; if he is thirsty, give him a drink" [Rom. 12:20]. Here no one can doubt that the verse is endorsing kindness.[28] But one would think that the following words, "for doing this you will pile coals of fire on his head," are advocating malicious wrongdoing. We can be sure therefore that it was meant figuratively. (*On Christian Teaching* 3.10.14; 3.11.17; 3.16.24; Green, *De doctrina christiana*, 147, 151, 157, modifed)

In an era that had few shared guidelines for interpreting different passages, Augustine's contributions to this end are significant. He writes *On Christian Teaching* knowing full well that he will be roundly criticized by fellow Christians for trying to encapsulate biblical meaning by resorting to a set of exegetical principles. They claimed that someone led by the Spirit will necessarily come upon the right interpretation because it is a gift of God. Augustine had no argument against the importance of being divinely illumined and directed when one is seeking to know the Bible's meaning. But he argued that such a view left to itself is an occasion for self-deception and arrogance. Besides, every person is in need of teaching that introduces the proper methods and procedures in order to learn how to speak and read. The same should apply to understanding Scripture.

L. Gregory the Great: Allegory Touches the Soul (ca. 590)

Allegory, after all, devises for the sake of the soul that is far removed from God, a stratagem that will elevate it to God. When the figurative language is interposed, the soul, even while it grasps in the words something on its own level, apprehends in their intelligible sense something that is not on its own level, and by earthly words is separated from what is earthly. . . .

The divine teachings are clothed in things that are familiar to us; the things out of which allegories are made. And as we consider the exterior words, we achieve an interior discernment. (*Exposition on the Song of Songs* 3; trans. Richard A. Norris Jr., trans. and ed., *The Song of Songs: Interpreted by Early Christian and Medieval*

28. Therefore, the passage is to be interpreted literally.

Commentators, The Church's Bible [Grand Rapids: Eerdmans, 2003], 8)

By the sixth century, Gregory, bishop of Rome, had inherited a rich legacy of biblical commentary that he could draw on for his own works of exegesis. Unfortunately, many of his expositions do not survive, except for sermons on the Gospels, on the opening and closing of Ezekiel, and two on Song of Songs (Solomon). Besides his massive commentary, *Moralia in Job*, one other work on 1 Kings is extant.

Gregory espoused a threefold approach to Scripture. In the letter which prefaced his Job commentary, Gregory compared the task of biblical interpretation to the building of a house: the literal or historical sense lays the foundation, the allegorical constructs the walls of the church's doctrine, and the moral adds the beauty of color over the whole structure.

The literal meaning should not be cast aside as unimportant; the literal or historical meaning of a passage could be perceived by anyone. Only a spiritually oriented believer can discern the spiritual depths that exist in the text. In so doing, the literal meaning was perfected by a spiritual understanding that draws the soul to God.

ALLEGORICAL AND SPIRITUAL INTERPRETATION

A. Paul the Apostle: The Prefigure of the Slave and Free

Tell me, you who want to be under the law, are you not aware of what the law says? For it is written that Abraham had two sons, one by the slave woman and the other by the free woman. His son by the slave woman was born in the ordinary way;[1] but his son by the free woman was born as the result of a promise.

These things may be taken figuratively [lit., allegorically],[2] for the women represent two covenants. One covenant is from Mount Sinai and bears children who are to be slaves. This is Hagar [Gen. 16:15]. Now Hagar stands for Mount Sinai in Arabia and corresponds to the present city of Jerusalem, because she is in slavery with her children. But the Jerusalem that is above [Heb. 12:22] is free, and she is our mother. . . .

Now you, brothers, like Isaac, are children of promise [Rom. 9:6–8]. At that time the son born in the ordinary way persecuted the son born by the power of the Spirit. It is the same now. But

1. Physically.
2. Though Paul's actual application of the word lends itself to "figuratively."

135

what does the Scripture say? "Get rid of the slave woman and her son, for the slave woman's son will never share in the inheritance with the free woman's son" [Gen. 21:10]. Therefore, brothers, we are not children of the slave woman, but of the free woman. (Gal. 4:21–26, 28–31)

B. Clement of Alexandria: Divine Things Known by Spiritual Knowledge (ca. 215)

The truly sacred Word, truly divine and most necessary for us, was deposited in the shrine of truth . . . [covered] according to the Hebrews by the veil. Only the consecrated—that is, those devoted to God, circumcised in the desire of the passions for the sake of love to that which is alone divine—were allowed access to them. For even Plato also thought it not lawful for "the impure to touch the pure." . . .

For this reason Paul says, "But we preach, as it is written, what eye hath not seen, and ear hath not heard, and hath not entered into the heart of man, what God hath prepared for them that love him. For God hath revealed it to us by the Spirit. For the Spirit searches all things, even the deep things of God" [1 Cor. 2:9–10]. For he recognizes the spiritual man and the gnostic[3] as the disciple of the Holy Spirit, bestowed by God, who has the mind of Christ. "But the natural man does not accept the things of the Spirit, for they are foolishness to him" [1 Cor. 2:14]. (*Miscellanies* 5.4; *ANF* 2:449, 450, modifed)

Clement was not a bishop but a leading catechist of the church of Alexandria. He was the teacher of Origen, among others, laying down a number of principles about the role of spiritual interpretation that Origen would utilize in his biblical commentaries.

C. Origen

1. Lifting of the Veil (ca. 225)

Now the light which was contained within the law of Moses, but was hidden away under a veil, shone forth at the advent of Jesus, when the veil was taken away and there came at once to men's

---

3. For Clement, the "gnostic" was a Christian who was spiritually enlightened or sensitized to the Spirit, different from an adherent of Gnosticism.

knowledge those "good things" of which the letter of the law held a "shadow."

It would require considerable labor if we were to record the time and manner in which every event predicted of old by the prophets has been fulfilled, in the hope that we might thereby confirm those who are in doubt; although it is possible for anyone who desires more accurate knowledge about these things to gather proofs in abundance from the books of the truth themselves. But if at first sight of the letter the superhuman meaning does not at once appear obvious to those who have been but little instructed in divine things, that is no wonder; because divine things are communicated to men somewhat obscurely and are the more hidden in proportion to the unbelief or unworthiness of the inquirer. For while it is certain that everything which exists or happens in this world is arranged by the providence of God, there are some things which show themselves quite plainly to be subject to the control of providence, whereas others evolve in a manner so obscure and so hard to understand that in their case the plan of divine providence is utterly concealed.

But just as providence is not lacking because of our ignorance, at least not for those who have once rightly believed in it, neither is the divine character of scripture, which extends through all of it, lacking because our weakness cannot discern in every sentence the hidden splendor of its teachings, concealed under a poor and humble style. For "we have a treasure in earthen vessels, that the exceeding greatness of the power of God may shine forth" and may not be reckoned as coming from us who are but men. (*On First Principles* 4.1.6–7; Butterworth, *Origen*, 265–67)

2. The Necessity of Spiritual Meaning (ca. 244)

For richly faceted and many textured is the planting of the words contained throughout all of Scripture. And as for the treasure that was hidden in the field [Matt. 13:44], this means the thoughts that are concealed and resting beneath what is plainly visible: namely, the thoughts of the wisdom concealed in a mystery and in Christ [1 Cor. 2:7], in whom are the concealed treasures of wisdom and knowledge [Col. 2:3]. (*Commentary on Matthew* 10.5; *ANF* 9:416)

For Origen, Scripture is simultaneously plain and mysterious because it was given by God's hand, who is himself both revealed and unfathomable. This double-sided character to Scripture is testimony to its divinity, though were it not for the depths of meaning that only the allegorical can bring, one would never grasp the true inspirational nature of the Bible, especially the Old Testament (*On First Principles* 4.1.6).

Both "sides" of the Bible are designed by God to work this way, marking the difference between the pagan or the carnal Christian from the spiritually sensitive believer who is making good progress in the Christian faith. In fact, the divine authors of the Bible are said to have purposely inserted "certain stumbling blocks, as it were" (such as contradictions or ethical inconsistencies) into the text, prompting the discerning reader to search for the hidden meaning (*On First Principles* 4.2.9). It follows that the hidden meaning will be concealed from many readers. Because "the Scriptures were composed by the Spirit of God, they have not only that meaning which is obvious, but also another which is hidden from the majority of readers" (*On First Principles* preface 8).

3. Contradictions Intentionally Placed in the Text (ca. 231)

But if in every detail of this outer covering, that is, the actual history and the sequence of the law, had been preserved and its order maintained, we should have understood the Scriptures in an unbroken course and should certainly not have believed that there was anything else buried within them beyond what was indicated at a first glance. Consequently the divine wisdom has arranged for certain stumbling blocks and interruptions of the historical sense to be found therein, by inserting in the midst a number of impossibilities and incongruities,[4] in order that the very interruption of the narrative might as it were present a barrier to the reader and lead him to refuse to proceed along the pathway of the ordinary meaning: and so, by shutting us out and debarring us from that, might recall us to the beginning of another way, and might thereby bring us, through the entrance of a narrow footpath, to a higher and loftier road and lay open the immense breadth of the divine wisdom. . . .

And we must also know this, that because the aim of the Holy Spirit was chiefly to preserve the connection of the spiritual meaning, both in the things that are yet to be done and in those which have already been accomplished, whenever he found that things which had been done in history could be harmonized with the spiritual meaning, he composed in a single narrative a texture comprising both kinds of meaning, always, however, concealing the secret sense more deeply. But wherever the record of deeds that had been done could not be made to correspond with the sequence of the spiritual truths, he inserted occasionally some deeds of a

---

4. In other words, a simple, literal reading of the scriptural text will show conflicts and contradictions that demand an allegorical or spiritual interpretation of the text.

less probable character or which could not have happened at all, and occasionally some which might have happened but in fact did not. Sometimes he does this by a few words, which in their bodily sense do not appear capable of containing truth, and at other times by inserting a large number.

This is found to happen particularly in the law, where there are many things which as literal precepts are clearly useful, but also a considerable number in which no principle of utility whatever is disclosed, while sometimes even impossibilities are detected. All this, as we have said, was supervised by the Holy Spirit, so that in those cases where the text at first glance appears to be neither true or useful, we should see the necessity for a deeper truth, requiring more careful examination. We ought to discover in the Scriptures, which we believe to be inspired by God, a meaning worthy of God. (*On First Principles* 4.2.9; Butterworth, *Origen*, 285–87, slightly revised)

4. Contradictions in the Literal Necessitate Spiritual Interpretation (ca. 231)

Although I have quoted the text of the Gospels at very great length,[5] I think this has been done necessarily to show the disagreement according to the literal meaning. The Synoptics[6] relate what most people assume to be the same things that are written also in John, to have occurred in one and the same visit of the Lord to Jerusalem. But John reports that the things related occurred in two ascents to Jerusalem separated by many acts revealed between them, and by visits of the Lord to different places.

I, therefore, assume that it is impossible for those who understand nothing beyond the historical meaning in these passages to show that the apparent disagreement is an agreement. And if anyone thinks that we have not understood it correctly, let him intelligently write a rebuttal to such a view as ours.

Now we shall set forth in the same manner, according to the ability given to us, the things which move us to the harmony of these texts, as we have asked him who gives to everyone who asks and struggles intensely to seek, and we are knocking, that the hidden things of Scripture may be opened us by the keys of knowledge [Matt. 7:7–8]. . . .

5. Origen is dealing with the Gospel texts that discuss Jesus's triumphal entry into Jerusalem.
6. Matthew, Mark, and Luke.

To perceive the meaning in these matters, therefore, belongs to that true understanding which has been given to those who say, "But we have the mind of Christ, that we may see the things that are given to us by God" [1 Cor. 2:16]. . . .

Jesus, therefore, is the Word of God who enters the soul, which is called Jerusalem, riding on an ass which has been loosed from its bonds by the disciples. Now by the ass I mean the artless letters of the Old Testament which are clarified by the two disciples who loose them. One of these disciples is the person who refers the things which have been written anagogically[7] for the service of the soul and who interprets words allegorically. For the other is the one who presents the good and true things, which are through those things found in the shadow.[8]

Now he is also riding the young colt, which is the New Testament. For it is possible to find in both Testaments the word of truth, which cleanses us and drives out all the arguments that are buying and selling in us.[9]

But he does not enter the soul, which is Jerusalem, alone; neither does he enter with a certain few. For there must be many things present in us which precede the Word of God who perfects us, and many others which follow him. All, however, praise and glorify him, and place their own clothing and garments under him, that his mounts might not touch the earth since they have the One who has come down from heaven resting upon them. (*Commentary on John* 10.129–31, 172–76; trans. R. E. Heine, FOC 80:285, 294–95)

5. Spiritual Harmony of the Four Gospels (ca. 231)

In the case of the four gospel writers, whom I have assumed wanted to teach us by a type[10] the things they had seen in their mind, if they should be wise, the meaning of their historical accounts would be found to be harmonious once it was understood. We must conceive that it is this way also in the case of the four evangelists who made full use of many things done and said in accordance with the prodigious and incredible power of Jesus. In some places they have interwoven in Scripture something made clear to them in a purely intellectual manner, with language as though it were something perceptible to the senses.

7. Anagogical statements are those whose meaning is determined by a mystical or spiritual interpretation.

8. The "shadow" is the reality we know in the world.

9. Manipulating us.

10. A figure that offers prophetic significance.

But I do not condemn, I suppose, the fact that they have also made some minor changes in what happened so far as history is concerned, with a view to the usefulness of the mystical object of [matters].[11] Consequently, they have related what happened in a certain place as though it happened in another, or what happened at this time as though at another time, and they have written down what was reported with a certain degree of distortion.

For their intention was to speak the truth spiritually and materially[12] at the same time where that was possible but when it was not possible to have it in both ways, to prefer the spiritual to the material. (*Commentary on the Gospel of John* 10.18–20; trans. R. E. Heine, FOC 80:259–60)

D. Hilary of Poitiers: Figurative Interpretation in the New Testament (ca. 350)

1. Reason for Peter's Sinking

There was a reason that the Lord did not grant to Peter in his fear the ability of reaching him, but extended his hand, thus catching him and holding him up: Peter was not yet worthy of approaching his Lord (for he had tried to draw near). At the same time, a typological pattern[13] has been observed in this situation.

The fact that the Lord walked upon the upheavals and storms of the world shows that no one is able to participate in his passion. He alone is going to suffer for all, and it is he who forgives the sins of all [Gal. 1:4]. Whatever is granted to the whole world is granted by the one who admits no associate. Thus, if he himself was the redemption of the entire world, he preserved Peter too—before he was to be redeemed—for that faith of redemption, even as a martyr of Christ. (*Commentary on Matthew* 14.16; SC 258:30, trans. D. H. Williams)

2. Canaanite Woman a "Type" of the Church

The Canaanite woman who confesses Christ as Lord and Son of David is not herself in need of healing but pleads on behalf of

---

11. Each evangelist slightly altered some parts of the Gospel account in order to make clearer the spiritual meaning. This is one reason why there are differences between the four narratives of Jesus's life and words.

12. Literally.

13. Latin, *typicus ordo*.

her daughter, that is, for the people of the pagans who have been weighed down by the domination of unclean spirits. The Lord says nothing in the forbearance of silence, reserving the privileges of salvation for Israel. And the disciples, feeling pity, join their supplication to the woman's. But he who comprises the mystery of the Father's will responds that he has been sent to the lost sheep of Israel, in order to make it absolutely clear that the daughter of the Canaanite woman represents a figure[14] of the church. While she sought what he had offered to others, not because salvation should not be bestowed on the pagans, but the Lord had come for his own and was waiting for the firstfruits of faith from among those he had been born. The others would later have to be saved by the apostolic preaching. (*Commentary on Matthew* 15.4; SC 258: 38, trans. D. H. Williams)

3. Blindness of the Pagans Brought to Sight

The two blind men sitting along the road are the two peoples of the pagans originating from Ham and Japheth. Upon learning of the Lord's passing by near them, they sought that their sight be restored to them [Matt. 20:29–34]. Then the crowd shouted them down because of their cries and told them harshly to be silent. This was not because the crowd regarded silence itself an honorable thing, but because they heard from blind men what they literally denied: the Lord is the Son of David. For having illuminated the minds of the blind, God in man was proclaimed; it was true when the Lord said: "For judgment I have come into this world that they who see not may see, and they who see might be made blind" [John 9:39].

"But they cried even more"; and although they were hindered by the people of the Law, they testified to the ardor of their faith more vehemently. But the Lord took pity and asked what they wanted. They asked that their eyes be opened. Having pity of them, he touched their eyes and restored their vision of the knowledge of God. And in order that a figure of those pagans who would believe may be fulfilled. They who had been blind, now having perceived the knowledge of heavenly grace, saw the Lord and followed him. (*Commentary on Matthew* 20.13; SC 258:118, trans. D. H. Williams)

14. Lit., a type.

In many passages of the Gospel, Hilary assumes that a double meaning exists within the text. The historical events themselves are recounted and can be taken literally. But often too there are "underlying causes that are prefigured" (*Commentary on Matthew* 14.3) in these events or characters which prompt a deeper or spiritual meaning. By "spiritual meaning" Hilary usually means figurative typology: the actions or personalities in the verse are representative of a future work of God. For Hilary spiritual exegesis was applied not merely to the Old Testament, but equally to the New Testament.

At the heart of the biblical text is a rationale or *ordo intelligentiae* (pattern of understanding) that is inherent to the verse. This means that exegesis is a process of unfolding the truth, almost always related to God's revelation in Christ whether for the present good of believers or, more often, for the future. It is particularly important to discover the *ordo* of a passage when the events as narrated seem self-contradictory or nonsensical. When a disciple sought that he be given time in order to bury his father, it was refused by Jesus, which prohibited the usual course of "human piety and service" [Matt. 8:21–22]. In defense, Hilary states, "The reason for such important and diverse events must be revealed because according to the order of events contained and the most profound causes of its truth, it is explained by an understanding of an interior significance" (*Commentary on Matthew* 7.8).

E. Ambrose of Milan: Three Kinds of Wisdom (ca. 388)

For there are three most excellent things that the philosophers of this world have considered to constitute a three-fold wisdom: the natural, the moral, and the rational. These three things are already evident even in the Old Testament. For what else do those three wells signify [Gen. 26:19–22, 33]—one of them being "vision," the second "abundance," and the third "oath"[15]—if not that a three-fold quality existed in the patriarchs? The rational well is "vision" because reason sharpens the mind's vision and cleanses the eye of the soul. The moral well is "abundance" because, once the foreigners had left (whose appearance symbolized the vices of the body), Isaac discovered the clarity of the living mind from which good morals flow forth purely. . . . The third well is "oath" . . . for what it asserts and promises—with God as its witness, so to speak—also embraces divine things, when the Lord of nature is cited as a witness to one's belief.

Therefore spiritual wisdom truly possesses every area that worldly knowledge falsely claims for itself, particularly inasmuch, to express ourselves rather boldly, our very faith, the mystery of the Trinity, cannot exist apart from this three-fold wisdom. We must

15. Or "Beersheba," the name Isaac gave to the place of the productive well (Gen. 26:33).

believe in that Father who of his *nature* begot for us the Redeemer; and in that *moral one* [16] who redeemed us, being obedient to his Father unto death [cf. Phil. 2:8] according to his humanity; and in that rational *Spirit* who instills in human hearts the grounds for the worship of God and governing our lives. (*Commentary on the Gospel of Luke*; B. Ramsey, trans., *Ambrose* [London: Routledge, 1997], 161–63, italics added)

The three kinds of wisdom Ambrose discusses (natural, moral, and rational) are the basis for three kinds of scriptural interpretation: the historical (literal), the moral, and the mystical (or allegorical). Not only were these three "senses" or meanings inherent to Scripture; these scriptural senses also reflected the very nature of God himself as Trinity.

While there was no one agreed-upon number of "senses" which could be found in the Bible, most patristic authors used a threefold (literal, moral, and mystical or spiritual) or fourfold (literal, moral, anagogical, and allegorical) approach. Even if the "senses" varied, the basic idea was the same: God had "built" these possible interpretations into the text for the edification and growth of his people.

F. Ephrem the Syrian: Depth of the Lord's Words (ca. 345)

If there were only one meaning for the words of Scripture, the first interpreter would discover it, and all other listeners would have neither the toil of seeking nor the pleasure of finding. But every word of our Lord has its own image, and each image has many members,[17] and each member possesses its own species and form. Each person hears in accordance with his capacity, and it is interpreted in accordance with what has been given him. (*Commentary on the Diatessaron*; McCarthy, *Saint Ephrem's Commentary*, 139)

Ephrem was the foremost writer within the Syriac Christian tradition in the fourth century. His hymns are best known for their formative influence on theological studies in the Syriac and Greek Christian communities. Indeed, Ephrem is among the few Syriac writers that later Greek historians include in their brief descriptions of important thinkers of the earliest centuries. Almost as important as his hymns were Ephrem's biblical commentaries,[18] one of which was on the second-century Gospel harmony of Tatian known as the *Diatessaron*.[19]

16. The Son.
17. Meanings.
18. Fragments of the Syriac text and a complete Armenian version survive.
19. Lit., "fourfold," for the four Gospels.

G. Augustine: Spiritually Interpreting "Light" and "Lights" in Genesis 1 (396–97)

So Lord, I pray you, as you are the Maker, as you are the Giver of cheerfulness and power, let "truth arise from the earth and justice look down from heaven" [Ps. 85:11], and let there be "lights in the firmament" [Gen. 1:14] . . . Let our light, which lasts but a short time, "break forth." Passing from the lower good works of the busy life to the delights of contemplation, may we "hold forth the word of life" [Phil. 2:16] by adhering to the "solid firmament" of your Scriptures.

It is your spiritual people established in the same solid firmament and distinguished by your grace who are manifested throughout the world. May they "give light over the earth and divide day and night and be for the signs of times" [Gen. 1:14].

"To one is given by the Spirit the word of wisdom" [1 Cor. 12:8], just like the "greater light" [Gen. 1:16] for the sake of those who delight in the light of truth as for "the rule of day." "To another is given the word of knowledge by the same Spirit," like "a lesser light"; and "to another faith, to another the gift of healings, to another miraculous powers, to another prophecy, to another the discernment of spirits, to another different tongues" [1 Cor. 12:8–10]. All these are like the stars. For "all these are the work of one and the same Spirit, dividing appropriate gifts to each person as he wills" [12:11]. He causes stars to appear manifestly for the advantage of all. But the "word of knowledge," containing all mysteries [13:2] and which varies at different times, is like the moon, and the other gifts recorded in the list just mentioned are like the stars. In principle, they belong to the "night," since they are inferior in brightness to the wisdom of the "day."

Even so they ("the lesser lights" or gifts) are necessary for those to whom I could not speak as if to spiritual persons, but as if to carnal. For wisdom is spoken among the perfect [2:6], but the "natural man" [2:14] is as an "infant in Christ" and a drinker of milk until he is strengthened for "solid food" [3:1–2; Heb. 5:12–14] and acquires eyesight strong enough to face the sun. Let him not think his "night" is destitute of all light, but be content with the light of the moon and stars. All these matters you set out most wisely with us, my God, through your book, your "solid firmament," so that we may discern everything by a marvelous contemplation, even though for the present, only by signs and times and days and years [Gen. 1:14]. (*Confessions* 13.18.22–23; H. Chadwick, trans., *Saint*

Augustine: Confessions [Oxford: Oxford University Press, 1986], 285–86)

Augustine's thirteenth and last book of the *Confessions* focused on interpreting Gen. 1–3 and served as a response against the Manichaean hyperliteral use of Genesis. But his rendering of Genesis, like a kind of allegorical template, also showed the major stages of Augustine's own life (creation, fall, and promise of redemption).

H. John Cassian: From the Desert Fathers: Wisdom about the Use of Scripture (ca. 420–29)

As the renewal of our soul grows by means of study, Scripture also will begin to put on a new face, and the beauty of holier meaning will somehow grow with our growth. For their form is adapted to the capacity of man's understanding, and will appear earthly to carnal people, and divine to spiritual ones, so that those to whom it formerly appeared to be involved in thick clouds, cannot apprehend its subtleties nor endure its light. (*First Conference of Abbot Nesteros* 14.11; *NPNF* 2/11:440)

The authority of Holy Scripture says on those points on which it would inform us some things so plainly and clearly even to those who are utterly void of understanding, that not only are they not veiled in the obscurity of any hidden meaning, but [also] do not even require the help of any explanation, but carry their meaning and sense on the surface of the words and letters: but some things are so concealed and involved in mysteries as to offer us an immense field for skill and care in the discussion and explanation of them. And it is clear that God has so ordered it for many reasons: first for fear lest the holy mysteries, if they were covered by no veil of spiritual meaning, should be exposed equally to the knowledge and understanding of everybody, i.e., the profane as well as the faithful, and thus there might be no difference in the matter of goodness and prudence between the lazy and the earnest: [the] next [reason is] that among those who are indeed of the household of faith, . . . there might be the opportunity of reproving the slothfulness of the idle, and of proving the keenness and diligence of the earnest. And so holy Scripture is fitly compared to a rich and fertile field. (*Second Conference of Abba Serenus* 8.3; *NPNF* 2/11:376)

Because there was no consensual method in interpreting Scripture, the patristic practice varied in its approaches. Different writers suggest three or four types of exegetical steps, more or less with the same end: the readers must not be bound to the literal or historical reading if they wish to discern God's teaching in the Bible. John Cassian, who spent several years among the desert ascetics in Egypt, returned to the West equipped with exegetical insights, which included a fourfold interpretive method. He found four levels of meanings in the Bible. Like most, Cassian distinguished between the historical (i.e., literal) and the spiritual, but he also identified three types of spiritual interpretation: *tropologica, allēgorica,* and *anagōgē.* By tropological, he meant moral interpretation; he understood the allegorical as typological, or figurative, exegesis (as in Gal. 4:24) and anagogical as the reference from earthly realities to heavenly ones.

I. Peter Chrysologus: Christ's Use of Mystical Interpretation (ca. 425)

The historical narrative of Scripture should always be raised to a higher meaning and the mysteries of the future should become known through figures of the present. Therefore, we should unfold by allegorical explanation what mystical teaching is contained beneath the outward appearance of the text.

When the Gospel text states, "He set a parable before them," it means that a potential spark is cold in the flint and lies hidden in the steel, but it is brought into flame when the steel and flint are struck together. In similar manner, when an obscure word is brought together with its meaning, it begins to glow.

Surely, if there were not mystical meanings,[20] no distinction would remain between the faithless and the faithful, between the wicked man and the devout one. The devout man would be like a proud one, the lazy man like a toiler, the watchful man like a sleeper. But, as things are, when the soul asks, the mind knocks, the power of perception seeks, piety hopes, faith demands, and studious attention deserves it, then, the one who labors in perspiration sees fruit appear. The lazy man, by contrast, is seen to suffer a penalty. This is why Christ veils his teaching by parables, covers it with figures, hides it under symbols,[21] and makes it obscure by mysteries. (*Sermon 36,* trans. George E. Ganss, FOC 17:48; and *Sermon 96,* FOC 17:152)

20. *Mystica,* meaning "symbolical" or "spiritual."
21. The Latin word is *sacramentis.*

THEOLOGICAL POETRY
AND HYMNS

A. Paul

1. Form of a Servant and of God

Your attitude should be the same as that of Christ Jesus:

Who, being in very nature God,
    did not consider equality with God something to be
    grasped,
but made himself nothing,
    taking the very nature of a servant [or slave],
    being made in human likeness.
And being found in appearance as a man,
    he humbled himself
and became obedient to death—
    even death on a cross!
Therefore God exalted him to the highest place
    and gave him the name that is above every name,
that at the name of Jesus every knee should bow,
    in heaven and on earth and under the earth,
and every tongue confess that Jesus Christ is Lord,
    to the glory of God the Father. (Phil. 2:5–11)

Perhaps the most striking example of the church's tradition in liturgical practice is the well-known christological passage of Phil. 2:5–11. In all likelihood, Paul has incorporated a previously known hymn (or fragment of a hymn) in order to illustrate his precept about putting the interests of others before our own (2:3–4). The New International Version has rightly set off the lines of this passage into stanzas. Whether the Philippians were previously familiar with the hymn is uncertain, but it seems that it was arranged in rhythmic strophes for purposes of congregational worship and instruction before it came into Paul's hands.

Typical of other christological formulas, the passage presents a condensed summary of Jesus's sacrificial death and Easter triumph. We discern a two-stage pattern: (1) Christ's humiliation as the obedient servant despite being in the form (*morphē*) of God, along with his incarnation and death and (2) his exaltation to the universally acknowledged position of Lord. The logic is evident: not through pretension but by sacrifice did Jesus demonstrate his true divine nature. Apart from the point as a whole, there is also the didactic value of each line, which builds a composite sketch of Christ's identity, whose preexistent and divine nature is the basis upon which the rest of the declaration is built.

2. The Mystery of Godliness

> He appeared in a body,
>   was vindicated by the spirit,
> was seen by angels,
>   was preached among the nations,
> was believed on in the world,
>   was taken into glory. (1 Tim. 3:16)

The poetic or hymnic origin of this passage becomes more evident when we observe that it is structured in three antithetical pairs as construed above. In each pair, a datum from the Jesus tradition is presented within a contrasting setting of the heavenly/spiritual and earthly/material. The focus is clearly on the process by which God revealed himself in Christ:

1. Related to the incarnation—God has come in the flesh/confirmed by the Spirit.
2. Related to the gospel proclaimed—testified by angels (at birth or resurrection)/preached among nations.
3. Related to the consequences of his coming—believed in the world/ascended to heaven.

The content of this hymnic confession is densely packed in a small amount of space, imparting crucial truths about the equal realities of Christ's physical appearance in the real world and his heavenly origin and purpose. In just a few lines, the faithful confess the universal nature of Christ's person while avoiding the extremes of exalting Jesus's divinity at the expense of his humanity—not an uncommon problem by the middle of the first century due to the influence of Gnosticism.

3. A Hymn of Confidence in Adversity

> If we died with him,
>   we will also live with him;
> if we endure,
>   we will also reign with him.
> If we disown him,
>   he will also disown us;
> if we are faithless,
>   he will remain faithful,
>   for he cannot disown himself. (2 Tim. 2:11–13)

Here is another instance of the apostle drawing upon an already-known liturgical source in order to substantiate his point. On this occasion, the emphasis is not centered on Christ. Paul is encouraging his young disciple to endure suffering, as he has, for the sake of the truth of the gospel. Above all, Timothy is asked "to remember" by invoking a form of the church's preaching that he was taught: "Remember Jesus Christ, raised from the dead, descended from David" (2:8). At this juncture, as Timothy is prompted to think back to the gospel tradition, which was the ground of his salvation, Paul introduces a "trustworthy saying" (*logos*) in four couplets, each beginning with the conditional particle *if*. The first couplet demonstrates the probability that the "saying" was part of a baptismal vow or a hymn sung at baptism.

The one being baptized is exhorted to endure and remain faithful by "living" in Christ. As a conditional vow, it is always possible for the new believer to "disown him" by rejecting their confession such "that sin may reign in the mortal body" (Rom. 6:12). And yet the graceful stability of God is not annulled in our moments of faithlessness, and the final note of the passage is to encourage rather than provoke.

B. *Psalms of Solomon*: Who Is Righteous? (end of 1st cent.)

> Why do you sleep, O soul, and do not praise the Lord?
> Sing a new song to God, who is worthy to be praised.
> Sing and know that he knows you,
>   for a good psalm to God is from a glad heart.
>
> The righteous remember the Lord always,
> acknowledging and proving right his judgments.
> The righteous does not lightly esteem discipline from the
>   Lord,
>   desiring always to be in his presence. . . .

The confidence of the righteous comes from God their Savior,
constantly removing sins from their house. . . .
Those who fear the Lord shall rise up to eternal life,
their life shall be in the Lord's light, and it shall never end.

(*Psalms of Solomon* 3.1–4, 6, 12b;
trans. R. B. Wright, *OTP* 2:654–55, modified)

The *Psalms of Solomon*, really the work of a Jewish Christian at the end of the first or the second century, appears in the fifth-century canonical list of Old Testament and New Testament books known as the Codex Alexandrinus.

C. *Odes of Solomon*: Praise for the Advent of the Messiah (early 2nd cent.)

1. *Ode 15*

As the sun is the joy to them who seek its daybreak,
so is my joy the Lord;

Because he is my sun, . . .
his light has dismissed all darkness from my face.

Eyes I have possessed in him,
and have seen his holy day.

Ears I have acquired,
and have heard his truth.

The thought of knowledge I have acquired,
and have lived fully through him. . . .

Eternal life has arisen in the Lord's land, . . .
and been given without limit to all that trust in him.

2. *Ode 29*

The Lord is my hope,
I shall not be ashamed in him.

For according to praise he made me,
and according to his grace even so he gave to me.

And according to his mercies he raised me,
and according to his great honor he lifted me up.

He caused me to ascend from the depths of Sheol,
and from the mouth of Death he drew me. . . .

For I believed in the Lord's Messiah,
and considered that he is the Lord.

And he declared to me his sign,
and he led me by his light.

3. Ode 41

Let all the Lord's babes praise him,
and let us receive the truth of his faith.

His children shall be acknowledged by him,
therefore let us sing by his love.

We live in the Lord by his grace,
and life we receive by his Messiah.

For a great day has shined upon us,
and wonderful is he who has given us of his glory. . . .

And let our faces shine in his light,
and let our hearts meditate in his love,
by night and by day.

Let us exult with the exultation of the Lord.

(*Odes of Solomon* 15.1–5, 10; 29.1–4, 6–7; 41.1–4, 6–7;
trans. J. H. Charlesworth, *OTP* 2:748, 761, 769)

The *Odes* are a Jewish-Christian compilation made at the end of the first or early second century AD and are, in effect, a collection of very early Christian hymns. They were not rediscovered and published until the beginning of the twentieth century.

D. Oxyrhynchus Papyrus 1786 (P.Oxy. 1786): The Earliest Christian Score of Music (later 3rd cent.)

Let it be silent
  Let the luminous stars not [shine,

Let the rushing winds cease (?) and] all
the roaring rivers. And as we hymn
the Father, the Son, and the Holy Spirit, let all the powers
add "Amen, Amen,"
might, praise [forever, and glory to God],
The sole giver of all good things, Amen. Amen.

> (B. P. Grenfell and A. S. Hunt, eds. and trans., *The
> Oxyrhynchus Papyri*, 55 vols. [London: Egypt Exploration
> Fund, 1898–15:1786)

P.Oxy. 1786 is one of hundreds of papyrus fragments found in a trash dump of the ancient city of Oxyrhynchus, Egypt, dating to the late third century. It is the only surviving score of Christian hymnody before the ninth century. The hymn, recorded on the back of a bill of lading for grain, is fragmented, consisting of five lines, with ancient Greek musical notation symbols written above the words. Whether the piece represents part of a hymn commonly used in worship by Egyptian Christians remains unclear. The fact that the score is found written on the back of a business record suggests it is a copy rather than the original.

E. Marius Victorinus: Theological Poetry (mid–4th cent.)

1. From the First Hymn

True Light, assist us,
O God the Father all powerful!
Light of Light, assist us,
mystery and power of God!
Holy Spirit assist us,
the bond between Father and Son!
In repose you are Father, in your procession, Son,[1]
And binding all in One, you are the Holy Spirit.

You yourself, O Father, are One, and One is the Son whom
    you beget.
For Christ as movement in repose is none other than God
    Supreme.
But when he is movement in movement, Christ is the Wis-
    dom and the Power of God,[2]

---

1. A key theme of Victorinus's works is a Stoicizing and Neoplatonic understanding of the Trinity as a movement of one being: the Father as repose or hidden motion, and the Son as externalized act of this motion.
    2. 1 Cor. 1:24.

In no way distant from the Substance, for movement is
  very substance.
And because this movement is in God and is very God,
It is called "God from God"[3] born,
however, because it is movement—for every movement is
  born—
and since God and the movement of God are One,
God and the movement of God are the one same God.

2. From the Second Hymn

Have mercy, Lord! Have mercy, Christ!
For I have believed in You.
Be merciful, Lord,
because through your mercy I have known You.

Have mercy, Lord! Have mercy, Christ!
You are the Word of my spirit,
You are the Word of my soul,
You are the Word of my flesh.

Have mercy, Lord! Have mercy, Christ!
Because God lives and God lives forever,
Hence life was born eternal,
But eternal life is Christ the Son of God.

Have mercy, Lord! Have mercy, Christ!
You who represent God the Father as the Begotten one,
Give me the keys of heaven
that I may rest in your place of light, saved by grace.

(Mary Clark, trans., *Marius Victorinus: Theological Treatises
on the Trinity* [Washington, DC: Catholic University of
America Press, 1981], 315–16, 320)

Victorinus was a pagan rhetor in the fourth century who converted late in life to Christianity. Augustine's work *Confessions* (8.2.3–4) recounts the story with the few details that are known. A total of three hymns are attributed to him, of which hymns 1 and 2 are fairly lengthy. Overall, the pieces strive to inculcate a pro-Nicene trinitarian thinking about God in poetic form. They are certainly less complicated than his prose works, which were said to be understood by few. Even so, his poems also retain some of the nuanced and philosophical teaching for which he became known in the West.

3. From the Nicene Creed.

F. Ambrose: Congregational Hymns (ca. 385)

1. "God, Creator of All Things"

God, Creator of all things
and Ruler of the heavens, fitting
the day with beauteous light,
and night with the grace of sleep.

Now the day is over and night begun,
we sing to you a hymn,
with thanks and asking that you loose us
from our sinfulness.

From the depth of our hearts, we praise you,
our ringing voices cry out to you,
with holy affection, we love you,
our ready minds adore you.

So when the deep gloom of night
closes in upon the day,
let our faith not know darkness,
and the night shine with hope.

As the depth of our heart casts aside unclean thoughts,
let it dream of you,
nor let worry of the enemy's schemes,
disturb us in peace.

We beseech Christ and the Father,
and the Spirit of Christ and the Father,
one power over all,
O Trinity, strengthen us we pray.

> ("Deus creator, omnium," Walpole, *Early Latin Hymns*, 46–
> 49; B. Ramsey, trans., *Ambrose* [London: Routledge, 1997],
> 170–71, slightly altered)

2. "Hearken, You, Who Rules Israel"

Come, Redeemer of the nations,
show to us the Virgin birth.
Let the whole world marvel,
such a birth should be worthy of God.

Not by a man's seed
but by the Spirit's mystic breathing,
did the Word of God become flesh
and the fruit of womb flourish.

. . . .

His going out is from the Father,
his coming is to the Father,
His journey as far as the grave,
his return is to the throne of God.

The equal of the eternal father,
he girds on the trophy of our flesh,
strengthening the frailty of our body
with his enduring strength.

May your crib now shine forth
and the night produce a new light,
that no darkness may dim,
and let it gleam with steadfast faith.

> ("Intende, qui regis Israel," Walpole, *Early Latin Hymns*,
> 52–57; C. White, ed., *Early Christian Latin Poets* [London:
> Routledge, 2000], 48–49, significantly altered)

According to Augustine (*Confessions* 9.6.14–7.15), Ambrose initiated the singing of hymns during church services in order to sustain the Milanese congregations emotionally and morally during the emperor Constantius's persecution of pro-Nicene loyalists in the paschal weeks of 385 and 386. Augustine's memories tell only part of the story. Ambrose had indeed made use of hymns to inculcate pro-Nicene doctrine among the people, given the pressure the emperor was bringing to bear on the Milanese church. It appears, however, that Auxentius, the Arian bishop before Ambrose, had introduced into congregational worship the use of hymns that he had brought with him from the East. In any case, hymns as teaching tools for sound doctrine and biblical understanding were becoming an important part of the church's way of teaching theology.

G. Hilary of Poitiers: Trinitarian Hymns (ca. 360)

1. A Hymn for the Morning

O wondrous Giver of light,
by whose illumination clear,
After the lingering hours of night,
the return of the day appears.

You are the True brightness of the world;
not like the insignificant sun [of the day]
That announces the coming of light,
shining with limited ray.

But brighter than the whole sun
is itself that perfect Light and its Day;
In our breast [just begun],
may you the heart illuminate.

Creator of all, be near!
You, the glory of the Father's light;
By whose grace you bear
that our being may be brought to sight.

This is the hope of the earnest soul,
a promised reward to impart.
That the morning may find in us
that Light, a guide through the dark.

Glory to you, Lord,
Glory to the Unbegotten,
with the Spirit Comforter,
now and forever more. Amen.

("Lucis largitor splendide," *PL* 10.551D–554B,
trans. D. H. Williams)

Medieval lore says he allegedly wrote this for his daughter Abra. Otherwise, nothing about its origin is known except that it has been attributed to Hilary.

2. *"An Ode to Christ the King"*

Let the faithful sing a hymn,
Let our song echo forth,
To Christ the King we render our debt of praises.

You are the Word
from the heart of God,
You are the Way, you are the Truth.

You are called the root of Jesse,
You are, we read, the Lion.

You are the Father's right hand, the Mount, the Lamb, the Cornerstone, the Bridegroom, God, the Dove, Fire, Shepherd, and the Door.

You, who were born into our world, are found in the prophets.
You, who were before all time, are the Maker of time's beginning.
You are the creator of heaven, of earth, gathering the seas.

You make the lame to walk, the blind to see the light.
You cleansed the leper by a word
and made alive the dead.

You commanded water to wine turn.
You fed five thousand with but five loaves, two fish,
in twelve baskets leftovers provided.

Let the faithful celebrate your glory,
which will remain with us, singing and entreating,
    throughout eternity,
together, let us celebrate the immensity of your majesty.

We sing to Christ the King, the Lord!

> ("Hymnum dicat turba fratrum," Walpole, *Early Latin Hymns*, 5–15, trans. D. H. Williams)

This selection is from a hymn attributed to Hilary in the hymnal of the ancient Irish church (Codex Aretinus). Hilary, bishop of Poitiers (died in late 360s), is one of the more colorful and prolific Latin authors in the mid-fourth century. For reasons not clear, Hilary was exiled to Asia Minor for three years, which opened his eyes to the doctrinal difficulties raging in the East and was just beginning to affect churches in the West. Through his correspondence and doctrinal works, he enabled churches in Gaul to understand what had been happening. Upon his return to Poitiers in the summer of 360, he finished the major work *On the Trinity* and resumed his pastoral duties, during which time, we presume, he composed the hymns.

H. Gregory of Nazianzus: Story of the Word Made Flesh (ca. 380)

Christ is born, give glory to him;
Christ comes from the heavens, gather to meet him;

Christ comes upon the earth, be filled with rejoicing.
"Sing to the Lord, all the earth" [Ps. 96:1],
and, since both heaven and earth are drawn together, I say,
"Let the heavens be glad, and the earth rejoice" [Ps. 96:11].
Through the heavenly and then the earthly spheres Christ
    is in the flesh;
exalt with trembling and with joy—
with trembling, because of sin,
with joy, because of hope.

Christ is come of a virgin.
First, without a mother.
Second, without a father.
The laws of nature are abrogated
that the cosmos above be brought to perfection.

Christ urges us, let us not resist;
"All you nations clap your hands" [Ps. 47:1],
because a child is born to us, a son is given to us.
Sovereignty is upon his shoulder (for he was raised up by
    the cross),
and his name is called Mighty Counselor (of the Father),
    Angel [Isa. 9:6].

Let John cry out, "Prepare the way of the Lord" [Matt. 3:3].
I, too, shall proclaim the power of the day.
The One without flesh has assumed flesh;
The Word has taken on materiality;
The Invisible had become visible;
The Impalpable is able to be touched;
The Timeless takes on a beginning;
The Son of God becomes Son of Man, Jesus Christ,
He who is yesterday, today, and forever [Heb. 13:8].

Hasten after the star, and offer gifts with the Magi,
gold, incense, and myrrh;
offer them to Christ
as king, the gold;
as him who died for you, the myrrh.
With the shepherds give glory,
with the angels hymn praise, join the choir of the
    archangels.

May there be common celebration in the powers of heaven
and earth.
I am convinced that the latter will join in the rejoicing
and the festive making today if indeed they are of good will
toward God and humankind, like those whom David
conducts after the passion of Christ.

They mount upward,
encouraging one another to lift up their gates [Ps. 24:7–9].
You are to detest only one aspect of the birth of Christ,
the massacre of the infants ordered by Herod.
Deplore this, the sacrifice of the children of the same age
as Christ;
they were sacrificed on behalf of the victim of the new age.
And when Christ flees to Egypt, call him out of Egypt,
rightly adoring him in that place.
As the disciple of Christ,
Pass blamelessly through all the stages of the life
and growing strength of Christ.
Be purified, circumcised, tear away the veil
surrounding you from your birth.
Then teach in the temple
and drive from the holy place the temple traders.
Suffer to be stoned, if it is necessary;
you will escape the stoners, I assure you,
and you shall flee through their midst, as God did,
for the Word is not to be stoned.
And if you are led before Herod, make little response.
He will be more shamed by your silence than by the wordi-
ness of others.
And if you are scourged, seek for what is still wanting.
Taste the gall for its bitterness;
don the scarlet robe, grasp the reed,
endure the worship of those who mock the truth.
Finally, allow yourself to be crucified, put to death, buried,
so that you may rise with him,
be glorified with him,
reign with him;
and, seeing God as he is, and being seen by him—
him who is adored and glorified in the Trinity,
him who is now to be made manifest to us,
him who is made accessible by the bonds of the flesh;
we pray

in Jesus Christ our Lord,
to whom is the glory forever. Amen.

(*Sermon 38*; Kannengiesser, *Early Christian Spirituality*,
78–81, slightly adapted)

Despite his deserved reputation as a theologian for the pro-Nicene position, Gregory of Nazianzus also published a series of poems, largely autobiographical in nature about his short-lived experiences as a bishop of Constantinople during the council of 381 and at Nazianzus.

I. Venantius Fortunatus: The Lord's Cross (6th cent.)

The blessed cross shines bright on which the Lord incar-
  nate hung,
And with his blood he washes our wounds,
Becoming for us a sacrificial offering, gentle in his devoted
  love.
The holy Lamb snatched the sheep from the wolf's jaws
When with hands transfixed he redeemed the world from
  disaster;
Blocking death's path by his own death.
Here was that hand pierced by the bloody nails,
The hand that snatched Paul from sin, Peter from death.
O sweet and noble tree, powerful in your fruitfulness,
Since you bear such fresh fruit on your branches.
This tree's new fragrance makes the corpses of the dead
  rise up,
And those who were deprived of the day return to life.
Summer's heat will not burn beneath the leaves of this tree,
Neither will the moon by night nor the sun at noon.
Planted beside the rushing waters you shine forth,
Spreading your leafy locks, adorned with fresh blossoms.
Between your arms, a vine is hung from which
There flow sweet wines, colored red as blood.

(*Poem* 2.1; Carolinne White, trans., *Early Christian Latin
Poets*, The Early Church Fathers
[London: Routledge, 2000], 165–66)

A sixth-century work written in northern Italy by the same author as for the panegyric *The Life of Hilary* (of Poitiers); and eventually he himself became the bishop of Poitiers.

FORMATION OF SCRIPTURE
AS CANON

A. The Muratorian Fragment (late 2nd or 3rd cent.)

The fragment begins with the last words of a sentence that obviously refer to Mark's Gospel. We can assume the missing material had to do with Matthew.

. . . But at some he was present, and so he set them down.

The third book of the Gospel according to Luke, was compiled in his own name on Paul's authority by Luke the physician, when after Christ's ascension Paul had taken him to be with him like a legal expert.[1] Yet neither did he see the Lord in the flesh; and he too, as he was able to ascertain events, begins his story from the birth of John.

The fourth of the Gospels was written by John, one of the disciples. When urged by his fellow disciples and elders,[2] he said, "Fast with me this day for three days; and what may be revealed to any of us, and let us relate it to one another." The same night it was revealed to Andrew, one of the apostles, that John was to write all things in his own name, and they were all to agree upon them.

1. Some conjecture that the term *iuris studiosus* means that Luke was an *adjutor*, an administrative assistant to Paul.

2. The word used here is an abbreviation of the plural for *episcopus*: a bishop, elder, or overseer.

And therefore, though various ideas are taught in the several books of the Gospels, yet it makes no difference to the faith of believers, since by one sovereign Spirit all things are declared in all of them concerning the nativity, the passion, the resurrection, the conversation with his disciples, and his two comings; the first in humility and contempt, which has come to pass, the second glorious with royal power, which is to come.[3]

It is not so amazing therefore if John consistently set forth each statement in his Epistles too, saying of himself, "What we have seen with our eyes and heard with our ears and our hands have handled, these things we have written to you" [1 John 1:1, 3–4]. For he declares himself to be not only an eyewitness and a hearer, but also a writer of all the miracles of the Lord in order.

The Acts of all the Apostles, however, are written in one book. Luke "to the most excellent Theophilus" [Luke 1:3], includes events because they were done in his own presence as he also plainly shows by leaving out the suffering of Peter, and also the departure of Paul from the city[4] on his journey to Spain.

The Epistles of Paul, however, themselves make plain to those who wish to understand them, what epistles were sent by him, and from what place or for what cause. He wrote at some length first of all to the Corinthians, forbidding the schisms of heresy; next to the Galatians, forbidding circumcision; then he wrote to the Romans at greater length, impressing on them the rule of the Scriptures,[5] also that Christ is the first principle of them, about which it is not necessary for us to discuss. For the blessed apostle Paul himself, following the rule of his predecessor John,[6] writes only by name to seven churches in the following order—to the Corinthians a first, to the Ephesians a second, to the Philippians a third, to the Colossians a fourth, to the Galatians a fifth, to the Thessalonians a sixth, to the Romans a seventh; although for the sake of admonition there is a second to the Corinthians and to the Thessalonians. Yet one church is recognized as being spread over the entire world. (For

3. It is noteworthy that the order of the Gospels listed above follows the conventional order of today's New Testament. A number of manuscripts put the order as Matthew, John, Mark, and Luke.

4. Perhaps indicating Rome. The use of "the city" was apparently familiar enough to the intended readership of this document and may be a clue to the author's location.

5. Not an unusual phrase for the early church, having to do with what principle(s) should be used for interpreting the Scripture. The writer typically claims that the rule is a christological one: the life, death, and resurrection of Christ are the means by which the believer should understand the Old Testament.

6. The apostle John may be Paul's "predecessor" in the sense that John was an apostle before Paul or that John's Gospel was understood to precede Paul's Epistles.

John too in the Apocalypse, though he writes to seven churches, yet is speaking to all of them.) Moreover, to Philemon one, to Titus one, and to Timothy two, which were put in writing out of personal affection and attachment. Nevertheless, these are in honor with the catholic church for the ordering of ecclesiastical discipline. There is in circulation also one to the Laodiceans, and another to the Alexandrians, both forged in Paul's name to suit the heresy of Marcion and several others.[7] These cannot be received into the catholic church; for it is not fitting that gall should be mixed with honey.

The Epistle of Jude, no doubt, and the couple bearing the name of John[8] are accepted in the catholic church; as well as the Wisdom written by the friends of Solomon in his honor.[9]

We receive only the Apocalypse also of John, and of Peter,[10] which some of our friends will not have read in church. But the Shepherd was written quite lately in our times in the city of Rome by Hermas, while his brother Pius, the bishop, was sitting in the chair of the church in the city of Rome; and therefore it ought indeed to be read, but it cannot always be publicly read in the church to the people, [as a book] either among the Prophets, who are complete in number, or among the Apostles.

But of Arsinous, called also Valentinus, or of Miltiades, we receive nothing at all. Those who have also composed a new book of Psalms for Marcion, together with Basilides and the Asian founder of the Cataphrygians are rejected.[11] (*The Fragment of Muratori*; Stevenson and Frend, *New Eusebius*, 123–24, modified)

This unique fragment was first published in 1740 by L. A. Muratori, who discovered it in the Ambrosian Library in Milan. While the anonymous author is not attempting to pose a theory about the scriptural canon, there is clear interest in what constitutes inspiration or the mark of divine authenticity, such as apostolicity, antiquity, and general acceptance by the churches. It is noteworthy that Hebrews, James, 1–2 Peter, and 3 John (?) are not mentioned, whereas the *Apocalypse of Peter* (questioned by some) and the Wisdom of Solomon are included. The fluidity of the Christian Scriptures is most apparent in this document. Many scholars place the

7. By the second century there was a proliferation of gnostic and Marcionite texts written in the name of Paul or another apostle.

8. Meaning 2 and 3 John if 1 John, quoted above, has already been recognized. Otherwise, 1 and 2 John are meant.

9. Patristic writers often cited the Wisdom of Solomon.

10. The *Apocalypse of Peter* was usually not accepted or read as Scripture in most churches. The author accepts it but acknowledges that others do not.

11. This is a blanket rejection of any additional "scriptural" writings produced by Gnostics, Marcionites, or Montanists (Cataphrygians).

original document to around 200, penned in Rome, though some have argued that the Greek original originated in fourth-century Palestine or Syria.

B. Melito of Sardis (ca. 190)

Melito to Onesimus, his brother, greetings. You have often requested, because of your enthusiasm for the word, that I send you extracts from the Law and the Prophets concerning our Savior and our faith as a whole. Moreover, you wanted also to learn the exact truth concerning the ancient books; what is their number, and in what order.

I was glad to perform such a task, knowing your enthusiasm for the faith and love for studying the Word, and that you, in your yearning for God, esteem these things above everything else as you contend for the prize of eternal salvation. After I went to the East and to the places where these were said and done,[12] I learned exactly which are the books of the Old Covenant,[13] of which I am sending you the list below:

Of Moses, five books: Genesis, Exodus, Numbers, Leviticus, Deuteronomy; Jesus Nave,[14] Judges, Ruth; four books of Kings; two of Chronicles, [the book] of Psalms of David, of Solomon, Proverbs, also called Wisdom, Ecclesiastes, Song of Songs, Job, of the prophets: Isaiah, Jeremiah, and the Twelve Prophets in a single roll, [and] Daniel, Ezekiel, Esdras. (from a book of *Extracts* recorded by Eusebius, *HE* 4.27.13–14; Lawlor and Oulton, *Ecclesiastical History*, 133, significantly modified)

Although Melito was a prolific author of some seventeen works, they now are all lost, except small excerpts such as the one above preserved in Eusebius of Caesarea's *Ecclesiastical History* and part of a work Melito wrote in Greek titled *On the Pascha* (see chap. 6.C, above).

C. Eusebius of Caesarea: How to Determine the Accepted Books (ca. 303)

We must then set in first place the holy foursome of the Gospels, which are followed by the book of the Acts of the Apostles. After

12. Melito's remark sounds as if he had made a pilgrimage to the Holy Land, where he visited the various important sites spoken of in the Old Testament. See the portion from Egeria's *Pilgrimage* (chap. 4.F, above); she made the same trip about 150 years later.

13. This is the earliest known reference to the Hebrew Scriptures as the Old Covenant (Testament).

14. Joshua.

this we must reckon the Epistles of Paul; following which we must pronounce genuine the extant former Epistle of John, and likewise the Epistle of Peter. After these we must place, if it really seems right, the Apocalypse of John, the views about which that have been held we shall set forth at the proper time.[15] These, then, are to be placed among the acknowledged writings. But of those which are disputed, nevertheless familiar to the majority, there is extant the Epistle of James, as it is called; and that of Jude; and the Second Epistle of Peter; and the Second and Third of John, so named, whether they belong to the evangelist or perhaps to some other of the same name as he.

Among the spurious writings there are to be placed also the book of the Acts of Paul, and the Shepherd, as it is called, and the Apocalypse of Peter; and, in addition to these, the extant Epistle of Barnabas, and the Teachings of the Apostles, as it is called; and, moreover, as I said, the Apocalypse of John, if it seem right. (This last, as I said, is rejected by some, but others give it a place among the acknowledged writings.) And among these some have reckoned also the Gospel of the Hebrews, a work which is especially acceptable to such Hebrews as received the Christ.

Now all these would be among the disputed writings; but nevertheless we have been compelled to make a catalogue of these also, distinguishing those writings which the tradition of the church has deemed true and genuine and acknowledged, from the others outside their number, which, though they are not canonical but even disputed, yet are recognized by most churchmen. [And this we have done] in order that we might be able to know both these same writings and also those which the heretics put forward in the name of the apostles, whether as containing gospels of Peter and Thomas and Matthias, or even of some others besides these, or as containing acts of Andrew and John and the other apostles. None of these has been deemed worthy of any kind of mention in a treatise by a single member of successive generations of churchmen; and the character of the style also is far removed from the apostolic manner, and the thought and purport of their contents is so absolutely out of harmony with true orthodoxy, as to establish the fact that they are certainly the forgeries of heretics. For this reason they ought not even to be placed among the spurious writings, but refused as altogether monstrous and impious. (*HE* 3.25.1–7;

15. Eusebius seriously doubted that Revelation should be placed among the "acknowledged" books and that John the apostle wrote it (*HE* 7.25.24–27).

Lawlor and Oulton, *Ecclesiastical History*, 86–87, capitalization adjusted)

Eusebius refers to the standard of accepted biblical books as "acknowledged" because there existed no one "canonical" list of books apart from what most of the churches had accepted as authoritative. Since there were differences among churches as to which books were acknowledged, Eusebius also recognizes the category of "disputed" books. In most cases, these books were read in the worship services of some churches as having value, though not the same authority as the "acknowledged."

D. Origen: The Complications of Many Gospels (ca. 245)

That there have been written down not only the four Gospels, but a whole series of gospels from which those that we possess have been chosen and have handed down to the churches. This is, let it be noted, what we may learn from Luke's preface, which runs thus: "For as much as many have taken in hand to compose a narrative" [Luke 1:1]. The expression "they have taken in hand" involves a implicit accusation of those who rashly and without the grace of the Holy Ghost have set about the writing of gospels.

Matthew to be sure, and Mark and John, as well as Luke did not "take in hand" to write, but filled with the Holy Ghost have written the Gospels. "Many have taken in hand to compose a narrative of the events which are quite definitely familiar among us." The church possesses four Gospels, whereas heresy has a great many, of which one is entitled *The Gospel according to the Egyptians*, and another, *The Gospel according to the Twelve Apostles*.[16] Basilides[17] also has presumed to write a gospel and to call it by his own name. "Many have taken in hand" to write, but only four Gospels are recognized. From these only the doctrines concerning the person of our Lord and Savior are to be derived. I know a certain gospel which is called *The Gospel according to Thomas* and a *Gospel according to Matthias*, and many others we have read. We do not in any way want to be considered ignorant because of those who imagine that they possess some knowledge if they are acquainted with these.[18] Nevertheless, among all these we have approved solely what the

16. Both texts, known as apocryphal gospels, survive.
17. A well-known teacher of Gnosticism that Origen mentions in other of his writings.
18. Accompanying the Gnostics' claims to possess other gospels was their assertion that those gospels provided a spiritual knowledge inaccessible to other Christians.

church has recognized, which is that only the four Gospels should be accepted. (*Homily on Luke* [1:1], according to the Latin translation of Jerome)

Origen also wrote commentaries on the Gospels according to Matthew and John. While Origen does quote from and refer to the *Gospel of Peter* and the *Gospel of the Hebrews*, he does not accord them the same authority as the four Gospels.

E. Cyril of Jerusalem: Advising New Christians about Biblical Parameters (ca. 350)

Of the Divine Scriptures. These are the things that we learn from the inspired Scriptures of the Old and the New Testament. For one God is the God of both covenants. In the Old Testament he foretold Christ as he appeared in the New, and was our schoolmaster leading us to Christ by way of Law and prophets. "For before faith came, we were kept under the Law" and "The law was our schoolmaster to bring us unto Christ" [Gal. 3:23–24]. And should you ever hear someone of the heretics blaspheming the Law or the Prophets,[19] cry out against him this saving phrase and say, "Jesus came not to destroy the law, but to fulfill" [Matt. 5:17]. And be studious to learn, and that from the lips of the church, all about the books of the Old Testament, and about those likewise of the New. But I charge you not to read any apocryphal book.[20] For while you remain ignorant of Scriptures that all confess to be inspired, why waste time on questionable reading? Read the divine Scriptures of the Old Testament, which is to say the twenty-two books interpreted by the two and seventy translators.[21]

For Alexander, king of the Macedonians, when he died, divided his kingdom into four dominions, the first of Babylonia, the next of Macedonia, then Asia, and last Egypt. One of the kings of Egypt was Ptolemy Philadelphus, a king very favorable to learning and a collector of all kinds of books. He heard from his chief librarian, Demetrius of Phalerum, of the divine Scriptures of the

19. Probably in reference to Marcionism, which denied the relevance of the Old Testament for claiming the Christian gospel.

20. The "apocryphal books" were those books that were not supposed to be read in the liturgy of worship.

21. That is, the Septuagint or "seventy volumes." Accounts of the origination of the Greek translation of the Old Testament sometime in the third century BC (first described in the *Letter of Aristeas*) vary between seventy and seventy-two translators. See comments at the end of this reading.

Law and the Prophets. He judged it to be the worthier course, by far, not to get possession of the books by force, from people who gave them up unwillingly, but to conciliate their possessors instead, with gifts and friendliness. He knew that what men surrender unwillingly under pressure they often spoil, whereas if it is forthcoming of the donor's free choice it is authentic throughout. So he sent off lavish presents to the temple then standing in Jerusalem, to Eleazar its high priest, and got him to send him six men out of each of the twelve tribes of Israel as translators. After that he conceived the idea of putting it to the test whether these books were divine scriptures or not. But he was suspicious lest the men sent from Jerusalem might put their heads together. So he assigned to each of the translators who had come to him his own private chamber in the quarter called Pharos in the vicinity of Alexandria. And there he ordered each of them to translate the whole Scriptures. The men completed their task in two and seventy days, all translating simultaneously in their separate chambers and without having any contact with one another. And when Ptolemy collected together all their translations, he found that they did not merely agree as to the meaning but were verbally identical. For what took place was not the result of sophistry, or contrived by human ingenuity. But just as Scriptures had been verbally inspired by the Holy Spirit, the Holy Spirit guided their translation.[22]

Read these twenty-two books, and do not have anything to do at all with the apocryphal writings. Give your earnest care to those books only which we read without hesitation in church. The apostles and the bishops who were set over churches in ancient times greatly excelled you, both in wisdom and piety, and they handed down these Scriptures to us.

If you are a son of the church, you must not modify their canon. And that, as I say, means reading carefully the twenty-two books of the Old Testament, and if you are ready, to learn them. I will say over their names, and you should try and commit them to memory. That is to say, in the Law the first are the books of Moses: Genesis, Exodus, Leviticus, Numbers, Deuteronomy; next, Joshua, the son of Nun, and then the book Judges, with Ruth, numbered as seventh. Of the remaining historical books, the First and Second Books of Kings count with the Hebrews as one book, and similarly

---

22. The account is meant to emphasize that nothing of the divine character of ancient Scripture was lost in its translation. The Greek version, therefore, was no less inspired than the Hebrew original.

the Third and Fourth Books. In the same way they count as one book First and Second Books of Chronicles. The First and Second Books of Esdras[23] are counted as one book, while Esther makes the twelfth; so much for the historical books. There are poetical books, Job, the book of Psalms, Proverbs, Ecclesiastes, and the Song of Songs as seventeenth book. In addition are prophetical books, that is one book of the Twelve Minor Prophets, one of Isaiah, one of Jeremiah with Baruch, Lamentations, and the Epistle to the Captivity,[24] then Ezekiel, and Daniel as the twenty-second book of the Old Testament.

Of the New Testament there are four Gospels only. All others are spurious and harmful. And the Manichees forged a *Gospel according to Thomas*,[25] which is smeared with the scent of the name of Gospel to murder the souls of those who are sufficiently foolish. Receive, however, the Acts of the Twelve Apostles, and the seven General Epistles of James, Peter, John, and Jude. The seal set upon them all and the latest work of disciples is the fourteen Epistles of Paul. Treat all other Christian writings as in a different class. And anything that is not read in the church do not you read privately, as you have already heard me say. And that is all, on that subject. (*Catechetical Lectures* 4.33–36; LCC 4:116–19)

In his instruction to catechumens, Cyril admonished them to read only those biblical books which are read in church (worship services), hence, the books deemed authoritative or "canonical." Thus, the meaning of "canonical" was not an a priori standard, but what the church observed in its practices of handling and interpreting the Bible.

This Jewish account about the origination of the Septuagint in one form or another was regarded as entirely historical and had proliferated within early Christianity from its beginning. Since the Greek Bible was for the most part the church's Bible, the story about the Septuagint's divine inspiration was readily received. For this reason, Latin translations were from the Greek version. In the early fifth century, when Jerome first made a new Latin translation of the Old Testament from the Hebrew (not depending on the Septuagint), many bishops and theologians, Augustine among them, refused to accept it (see *On Christian Teaching* 2.15.22).

23. Ezra and Nehemiah.

24. The Epistle of Jeremiah to the Captivity, which is the sixth chapter of the book of Baruch.

25. The *Gospel of Thomas*, already known by the second century, was not produced by the Manichees, a sect that originated in Persia and had spread to the Roman Empire by the end of the third century. Because Thomas has some gnostic characteristics, it was assumed to have come from Manichaean circles, both sharing radical dualism and christological docetism.

F. Athanasius of Alexandria: *Festal Letter 39* (announcing April 1 as the date for celebrating Easter in the year 367)

Inasmuch as some have taken in hand to draw up for themselves an arrangement of the so-called apocryphal books and to intersperse them with the divinely inspired Scripture, concerning which we have been fully persuaded, even as those who from the beginning were eyewitnesses and ministers of the word delivered it to the fathers: it has seemed good to me also, having been stimulated thereto by true brethren, to set forth in order the books which are included in the canon and have been delivered to us with accreditation that they are divine. My purpose is that each one who has been led astray may condemn those who have led him astray and that those who have remained untarnished may rejoice at having these things brought to remembrance again.

The books of the Old Testament, then, are twenty-two in number, for (as I have heard) this is the traditional number of [alphabetical] letters among the Hebrews. The first is Genesis, then Exodus, next Leviticus, after that Numbers, and then Deuteronomy. Following these there is Joshua, the son of Nun, then Judges and Ruth. And after these, the four books of the Kings, the first and second being reckoned as one book and so likewise the third and fourth as one book. And again, the first and second of Chronicles are reckoned as one book. Again, Ezra, the first and second[26] are similarly one book. After these there is the book of Psalms, then the Proverbs, next Ecclesiastes, and the Song of Songs. Job follows, then the Prophets, the Twelve being reckoned as one book. Then Isaiah, one book, then Jeremiah with Baruch, Lamentations, and the epistle, one book.[27] Afterwards, Ezekiel and Daniel, each one book. Thus far constitutes the Old Testament.

Again, it is not tedious to name the books of the New Testament. They are as follows: Four Gospels—according to Matthew, according to Mark, according to Luke, according to John.

Then after these Acts of the Apostles and the seven so-called Catholic Epistles of the apostles, as follows: one of James, two of Peter, three of John and, after these, one of Jude.

Next to these are fourteen Epistles of the apostle Paul, written in order as follows: First, to the Romans; then two to the Corinthians, and after these to the Galatians and next that to the Ephesians;

26. Ezra and Nehemiah.
27. Baruch 6 and the Letter of Jeremiah were counted as part of Jeremiah.

then to the Philippians and one to the Colossians and two to the Thessalonians and that to the Hebrews. Next are two to Timothy, one to Titus, and last the one to Philemon.

Moreover, John's Apocalypse.[28]

These are the "springs of salvation" [Isa. 12:3], so that one who is thirsty may be satisfied with the oracles which are in them. In these alone is the teaching of true religion proclaimed as good news. Let no one add to these or take anything from them. For concerning these our Lord confounded the Sadducees when he said, "You are wrong because you do not know the scriptures" [Matt. 22:29]. And he reproved the Jews, saying, "You search the scriptures, because . . . it is they that bear witness to me."

But for the sake of greater accuracy I must needs, as I write, add this: there are other books outside these, which are not indeed included in this canon, but have been appointed from the time of the fathers to be read to those who are recent converts to our company and wish to be instructed in the word of true religion. These are . . . the so-called *Teaching of the Apostles* and the *Shepherd*.[29] But while the former are included in the canon and the latter are read [in church], no mention is to be made of the apocryphal works. They are the invention of the heretics, who write according to their own will, and gratuitously assign and add to them dates so that, offering them as ancient writings, they may have an excuse for leading the simple astray. (*Festal Letter* 39.3–4; *NPNF* 2/4:551–52, capitalization adjusted)

Athanasius wrote a pastoral letter at Easter time to his congregation every year he served as bishop, and most of these have survived in Coptic or Syriac. In his letter issued in the year 367, Athanasius discussed which books ought to be regarded as read authoritatively in church (canonical).

G. Earliest Known Latin Conciliar[30] List of Scripture (382)

It is necessary to deal with the divine scriptures, which the universal catholic church accepts and which it should avoid.

28. A reference to the book of Revelation, which was generally not accepted in Greek churches, as well as to the many other gospels and acts allegedly written by other apostles.

29. The *Didache* and the *Shepherd of Hermas* were counted as canonical Scripture in other churches.

30. That is, from a council.

This is the order of the Old Testament:

Genesis	one book
Exodus	one book
Leviticus	one book
Numbers	one book
Deuteronomy	one book
Joshua	one book
Judges	one book
Ruth	one book
Kings	four books[31]
Chronicles	two books
150 Psalms	one book

Of Solomon:

Proverbs	one book
Ecclesiastes	one book
Song of songs	one book
Also, Wisdom	one book
Ecclesiasticus	one book

Likewise the order of the prophets:

Isaiah	one book
Jeremiah	one book
with Cinoth, i.e., his	
lamentations[32]	
Ezekiel	one book
Daniel	one book
Hosea	one book
Amos	one book
Micah	one book
Joel	one book
Obadiah	one book
Jonah	one book
Nahum	one book
Habbakuk	one book
Zephaniah	one book
Haggai	one book

31. The equivalent of 1 and 2 Samuel and 1 and 2 Kings.
32. The book of Lamentations has usually been attributed to Jeremiah. "Cinoth" is Latin for "ashes."

Zechariah	one book
Malachi	one book

Likewise the order of the histories:

Job	one book
Tobit	one book
Esdras	two books
Esther	one book
Judith	one book
Maccabees	two books

Likewise the order of the Scriptures of the new and eternal testament which the holy and catholic Roman church accepts:

Of the Gospels:

according to Mathew	one book
according to Mark	one book
according to Luke	one book
according to John	one book

The letters of the apostle Paul in number fourteen:

to the Romans	one
to the Corinthians	two
to the Ephesians	one
to the Thessalonians	two
to the Galatians	one
to the Philippians	one
to the Colossians	one
to Timothy	two
to Titus	one
to Philemon	one
to the Hebrews	one

Likewise the Apocalypse of John, one book

And the Acts of the Apostles, one book

Likewise the canonical letters, seven in number

of the apostle Peter	two letters
of the apostle James	one letter

of the apostle John	one letter
of the other John, the elder	two letters
of the apostle Judas, the Zealot	one letter

Here ends the canon of the new testament.

> (Latin text in C. H. Turner, "Latin Lists of the Canonical Books: 1. The Roman Council under Damasus, A.D. 382," *Journal of Theological Studies* 1 [1899–1900]: 557–59, trans. D. H. Williams)

Though re-edited in later centuries, the above list is associated with a council held in Rome during 382. The document issued by the council begins: "Here begins the council of Rome under Pope Damasus on explaining the faith." It was unusual for a council to define an authoritative list of scriptural books.

H. Jerome

1. On the Revision of the Latin Bible (383)

You[33] urge me to make a new work out of an old one,[34] and as it were, to sit in judgment on the copies of the Scriptures now scattered throughout the whole world, and since they differ from one another, to decide which of them agree with the true reading of the Greek original. The labor is one of love, but at the same time both perilous and presumptuous; for, in judging others, I must be myself judged by all; and how can I dare to change a language that is old and carry the world back in its hoary old age to the early days of its infancy? Is there a man, learned or unlearned, who will not, when he takes the volume into his hands, and perceives that what he reads does not suit his settled tastes, break out immediately into violent language, and call me a forger and a profane person for having the audacity to add anything to the ancient books, or to make any changes or corrections therein? So there are two consoling reflections that enable me to bear the odium—in the first place, the command is given by you who are the supreme bishop; and, second, even on the showing of those who revile us,

33. Damasus, bishop of Rome.
34. This preface marks the beginning of Jerome's work translating from the Hebrew and Greek into Latin. Jerome did indeed fulfill his task to a large extent; the OT and the Gospels are securely attributed to him, though how much more of NT he did is not clear. This version has gone by the name of the *Vulgata*, or common version, the Latin Vulgate.

readings at variance with the early copies cannot be right. For if we are to pin our faith to the Latin texts, it is for our opponents to tell us *which*; for there are almost as many forms of texts as there are copies. If, on the other hand, we are to glean the truth from a comparison of many, why not go back to the original Greek and correct the mistakes introduced by inaccurate translators, and the blundering alterations of confident but ignorant critics, and further all that has been inserted or changed by copyists more asleep than awake?

Speaking of the New Testament, it was undoubtedly composed in Greek, with the exception of the work of Matthew the Apostle, who was the first to commit to writing the Gospel of Christ, and who published his work in Judea in Hebrew characters. We must confess that as we have it in our language[35] it is marked by discrepancies, and now that the stream is distributed into different channels,[36] we must go back to the fountainhead. (*Preface to the Four Gospels*; CCC, 183, slightly modified)

I am not so ignorant as to suppose that any of the Lord's words is either in need of correction or is not divinely inspired; but the Latin manuscripts of the Scriptures are proved to be faulty by the variations which all of them exhibit, and my object has been to restore them to the form of the Greek original, from which my detractors do not deny that they have been translated. (*Epistle* 27; CCC, 184)

2. Instructions for a Young Woman's Education (403)

Let her treasures be not silks or gems but manuscripts of the Holy Scriptures; and in these let her think less of gilding, and Babylonian parchment, and arabesque patterns, than of correctness and accurate punctuation. Let her begin by learning the Psalter,[37] and then let her gather rules of life out of the Proverbs of Solomon. From the Preacher let her gain the habit of despising the world and its vanities.[38] Let her follow the example set in Job of virtue and of patience. Then let her pass on to the Gospels never to be laid aside when once they have been taken in hand. Let her also drink in with a willing heart the Acts of the Apostles and the Epistles.

35. There were various translations of the Bible in Latin by Jerome's time and would continue to be so even after the Vulgate was released.
36. There were various editions of the New Testament in circulation.
37. The Psalms.
38. Ecclesiastes.

As soon as she has enriched the storehouse of her mind with these treasures, let her commit to memory the Prophets, the Heptateuch,[39] the books of Kings and of Chronicles, the rolls also of Ezra and Esther. When she has done all these, she may safely read the Song of Songs but not before, because were she to read it at the beginning, she would fail to perceive that, though it is written in fleshly words, it is a marriage song of a spiritual bride. And not understanding this, she would be hurt from it.

Let her avoid all apocryphal writings, but if she is led to read these not for the truth of the doctrine they contain, but out of respect for the miracles contained in them, let her understand that they are not really written by those to whom they are ascribed.[40] Because many faulty elements have been introduced into them, it requires infinite discretion to look for gold in the midst of dirt.

Cyprian's writings[41] let her have always in her hands. The letters of Athanasius[42] and the treatises of Hilary[43] she may go through without fear of stumbling. Let her take pleasure in the works and wits of all in whose books a due regard for the faith is not neglected. But if she reads the works of others, let it be rather to judge them than to follow them. (*Epistle* 107.12; *NPNF* 2/6:194, modified)

The above is part of a longer letter that Jerome wrote Laeta in response to her request for advice about how she should best educate her young daughter, Paula. In effect, Jerome's answer provides a narrative description of the scriptural canon as well as some of the influential thinkers from the third and fourth centuries. While he is not saying that early fathers are equal in authority to Scripture, it is insinuated that they provide the best examples for how the Scripture is to be used in pastoral and polemical situations.

I. Augustine

1. When Doubts Are Raised about Which Books Are Canonical (ca. 396)

Now you see the strength of the authority of the catholic church, which is solidly supported by a succession of bishops from the

39. I.e., Genesis, Exodus, Leviticus, Numbers, Deuteronomy, Joshua, and Judges.

40. I.e., *Gospel of Peter, Gospel of Thomas, Acts of Paul, Apocalypse of Peter*, etc. These pseudonymous works, which come from the second and third centuries, emphasize the miraculous powers of Jesus or of the apostles.

41. Cyprian of Carthage, bishop of Carthage, was martyred in 257.

42. Athanasius of Alexandria (d. 373) left a large body of polemical works and Easter letters that he wrote to his congregation every year (see 9.F, above).

43. Hilary of Poitiers, bishop and articulate defender of a pro-Nicene trinitarian theology.

foundation provided by the apostles until the present time, and by the consensus of the people. Also, if the faith in certain merited [scriptural] texts was doubted, which has been the case upon occasion—though these variations are not numerous and are well known to those versed in Scripture—we then refer to the manuscripts of the area[44] from which the teaching came to clarify these inconsistencies. And if the manuscripts were not in agreement upon a variant text, we accord greater authority to the version which had greater support [among the churches], and prefer the older to the newer. And if uncertainty still remained about the variation, one would consult the text in its original language. This is how we seek to clarify points that confront us in Scripture and so provide a solid base of authority for proceeding [to an interpretation]. (*Against Faustus* 11.2; *NPNF* 1/4:178, significantly modifed)

For the canonical books [are], moreover, invested with authority by so many catholic churches, among which one finds without a doubt churches that were privileged to be apostolic sees and receive their writing from the apostles. This is the principle that one should follow in the inventory of these books: Those which are accepted by the whole of catholic churches will be placed before those writings which some [churches] do not accept. Concerning the issue of books that are not universally accepted, those which are admitted by the largest number of churches and the most important churches will be placed before those which are admitted by fewer churches and churches of less authority. Finally, there are certain books that are accepted by the majority of churches and some others that are accepted by important churches, in these cases I deem that both must be given the same authority. (*On Christian Teaching* 2.8.12; *NPNF* 1/2:538, significantly modified)

2. Those Books Accepted by Most of the Churches (396)

In the matter of canonical scriptures we should follow the authority of as many catholic churches as possible, including of course those that were found worthy to have apostolic seats and receive apostolic letters. We will apply this principle to the canonical scrip-

---

44. There was a sizeable number of Latin versions of the Scriptures available since the second century (as there were Greek), just as Augustine once exclaimed: "The Latin translators are beyond counting. In the early days of the faith, every person who happened to get possession of a Greek manuscript and imagined he had any facility in both languages, however slight that may have been, dared to make a translation" (*On Christian Teaching* 2.11.16).

tures: to prefer those accepted by all catholic churches to those which some do not accept. As for those not universally accepted, we should prefer those accepted by a majority of churches, and by the more authoritative ones, to those supported by fewer churches, or by churches of lesser authority. Should we find that some scriptures are accepted by the majority of churches, but others by the more authoritative ones[45] (though we could not possibly find this situation), I think that they should be considered to have equal authority.

The complete canon of scripture, on which I say that our attention should be concentrated, includes the following books: the five books of Moses (Genesis, Exodus, Leviticus, Numbers, Deuteronomy), and the single books of Joshua son of Nave and of Judges, and the little book known as Ruth, which seems to relate more to the beginning of Kings, and then the four books of Kings and the two of Chronicles, which do not follow chronologically but proceed as it were side by side with Kings. All this is historiography, which covers continuous periods and gives a chronological sequence of events. There are others, forming another sequence, not connected with either this class or each other, like Job, Tobias, Esther, Judith, and the two books of the Maccabees and the two of Ezra,[46] which rather seem to follow on from the chronologically ordered account which ends with Kings and Chronicles. Then come the prophets, including David's single book of Psalms, and three books of Solomon, namely, Proverbs, Song of Songs, and Ecclesiastes. The two books entitled Wisdom and Ecclesiasticus are also said to be by Solomon, on the strength of a general similarity; but there is a strong tradition that Jesus Sirach wrote them, and, in any case, because they have been found worthy of inclusion among authoritative texts, they should be numbered with the prophetic books. There remain the books of the prophets properly so called, the individual books of the twelve prophets who because they are joined together and never separated are counted as one. Their names are these: Hosea, Joel, Amos, Obadiah, Jonah, Micah, Nahum, Habakkuk, Zephaniah, Haggai, Zachariah, and Malachi. Then there are the four prophets in larger books: Isaiah, Jeremiah, Daniel, Ezekiel. These forty-four books form the authoritative Old Testament.[47]

45. These would be the metropolitan churches: Carthage, Rome, Milan, etc.
46. Ezra and Nehemiah.
47. As based on the Septuagint, which Augustine calls "supreme" among the many versions of the Old Testament available in his day. Augustine accepts the account of the seventy translators who are said to "have performed their task of translation with such

The authoritative New Testament consists of the Gospel in four books (Matthew, Mark, Luke, John), fourteen letters of the apostle Paul (Romans, Corinthians [two], Galatians, Ephesians, Philippians, Thessalonians [two], Colossians, Timothy [two], Titus, Philemon, Hebrews), two of Peter, three of John, one of Jude, and the one of James, the single book of the Acts of the Apostles and the single book of the Revelation of John.

These are all the books in which those who fear God and are made docile by their holiness seek God's will. The first rule in this laborious task is, as I have said, to know these books; not necessarily to understand them but to read them so as to commit them to memory or at least make them not totally unfamiliar. Then the matters which are clearly stated in them, whether ethical precepts or articles of belief, should be examined carefully and intelligently. The greater a person's intellectual capacity, the more of these he finds. In clearly expressed passages of scripture one can find all the things that concern faith and the moral life (namely hope and love, treated in my previous book). Then, after gaining a familiarity with the language of the divine scriptures, one should proceed to explore and analyze the obscure passages, by taking examples from the more obvious parts to illuminate obscure expressions, and by using the evidence of indisputable passages to remove the uncertainty of ambiguous ones. Here memory is extremely valuable; and it cannot be supplied by these instructions if it is lacking. (*On Christian Teaching* 2.8.12–2.9.14; Green, *De doctrina christiana*, 67–71)

J. Regulations for Pastors and Laity in the Church (late 4th–early 5th cent.)

Let the following books be regarded as venerable and holy by you, both of the clergy and laity. Of the Old Testament: the five books of Moses—Genesis, Exodus, Leviticus, Numbers, and Deuteronomy; one of Joshua the son of Nun, one of the Judges, one of Ruth, four of the Kings, two of the Chronicles, two of Ezra, one of Esther, one of Judith, three of the Maccabees, one of Job, one hundred and fifty psalms; three books of Solomon—Proverbs, Ecclesiastes, and the Song of Songs; as well as the sixteen prophets. And besides

---

strong guidance by the Holy Spirit that this large number of men spoke with but a single voice" (*On Christian Teaching* 2.15.22).

these, take care that your young persons learn the Wisdom of the very learned Sirach.

But our sacred books, that is, those of the New Covenant, are these: the four Gospels of Matthew, Mark, Luke, and John; the fourteen Epistles of Paul; two Epistles of Peter, three of John, one of James, one of Jude; two Epistles of Clement; and the Constitutions dedicated to you the bishops by me Clement, in eight books; which it is not fit to publish before all, because of the mysteries contained in them; and the Acts of us the Apostles. (*Apostolic Constitutions: Ecclesiastical Canons* 85; *ANF* 7:505)

The *Apostolic Constitutions* is a notoriously hard document to date because, even though it claims to be written in the first century by the same Clement mentioned by Paul in Phil. 4:3, it is really a composite work made up of later texts, placing it in the late fourth or early fifth century. The above list of books shows that the writer was dependent upon the Greek Bible for his knowledge of the Old Testament. For the New Testament, the postapostolic texts known as *1 Clement* and *2 Clement* are included, as they were in some canonical lists of Scripture. Unique and suspicious to the catalogue is Pseudo-Clement's inclusion of his own eight books of *Apostolic Constitutions*.

K. Pseudo-Athanasius: *Synopsis of Sacred Scripture* (ca. 495)

All divinely inspired Scripture belongs to us Christians. The books are not undefined but defined, and have canonical status. The books of the Old Testament are of Moses: Genesis, . . . Exodus, . . . Leviticus, . . . Numbers, . . . Deuteronomy, . . . Jesus, Son of Nave, . . . Judges, . . . Ruth, . . . First and Second Kingdoms, . . . Third and Fourth Kingdoms, First and Second Paralipomenon, . . . First and Second Esdras, . . . the Davidic Psalter, . . . the Proverbs of Solomon, . . . Ecclesiastes, . . . Canticle of Canticles, . . . Job, . . . the Twelve Prophets in one book: . . . Osee, . . . Amos, . . . Micheas, . . . Joel, . . . Abdias, . . . Jonas, . . . Nahum, . . . Habacuc, . . . Sophonias, . . . Aggeus, . . . Zacharias, . . . Malachias. . . . These are the twelve Prophets in one book, besides which there are four others: . . . Isaias, . . . Jeremias, . . . Ezechiel, . . . Daniel. . . .

The canonical books of the Old Testament are therefore twenty-two in number, equal in number to the letters of the Hebrew alphabet. Besides these there are also other books of the same Old Testament, which are not canonical, and which are read only to the catechumens.[48] These are the Wisdom of Solomon, . . . the Wisdom of Jesus, Son of Sirach, . . . Esther, . . . Judith, . . . Tobias. . . . These are not canonical. So much then for the books of the Old Testament, both the canonical and the noncanonical.

Of the New Testament the defined and canonical books are these: Matthew, . . . Mark, . . . Luke, . . . John, . . . Acts of the Apostles. . . . The Catholic Epistles of various Apostles are seven in number, enumerated in one book: one of James, . . . two of Peter, . . . three of John, . . . one of Jude. . . . Of the Apostle Paul there are fourteen epistles enumerated in one book: first, to the Romans, . . . two to the Corinthians, . . . fourth, to the Galatians, . . . fifth, to the Ephesians, . . . sixth, to the Philippians, . . . seventh, to the Colossians, . . . two to the Thessalonians, . . . tenth, to the Hebrews, . . . two to Timothy, . . . thirteenth, to Titus, . . . fourteenth, to Philemon, . . . Besides these there is also the Apocalypse of John the Theologian. . . . These are the canonical books of the New Testament. (*Synopsis of Sacred Scripture*; W. A. Jurgens, ed. and trans., *The Faith of the Early Fathers* [Collegeville, MN: Liturgical Press, 1970], 3:255–56)

This work has been preserved among the writings of Athanasius, but it is clearly not written by Athanasius, nor does it match the list of books that Athanasius names in his *Festal Letter 39*. Dating from the closing years of the fifth century, the *Synopsis* is considerably more than a canonical list. It provides the opening line of each book of Scripture and a brief digest of the contents of each book, which is not included above.

The above canonical list shows the consistency now present between such collections of biblical books. Still, there are points of difference. Esther is listed among the noncanonical books, and noncanonical books were considered valuable in the church in providing profitable instruction for catechumens. The Apocalypse, or Revelation, is associated not with the apostle John but with another John (a point generally accepted in the East), and the Pauline texts are listed after the Catholic Epistles. Hebrews is typically placed under Paul's name.

---

48. "Read only to the catechumens" means that these books do contain value for Christian instruction (doctrinal and moral), but they were not to be read in church as carrying the same authority as the "canonical."

APPENDIX

Scriptural References behind the Niceno–Constantinopolitan Creed

T HE SERIOUSNESS WITH which the early fathers formulated creeds in the light of scriptural teaching and actual wording is made apparent from one of the best-known creeds listed below.[1] Many other references may be found and applied to each of the stanzas, as could be done to all the major (and minor) creeds.

We believe in	Rom. 10:8–10; John 14:1
one God	Deut. 6:4, Eph. 4:6
the Father	Matt. 5:16; 6:9; Phil. 2:11
Almighty,	Gen. 17:1; Exod. 6:3; Rev. 19:15
maker of heaven and earth,	Gen. 1:1; Isa. 42:5
and of all things visible and invisible;	Eph. 1:10; Col. 1:16
and in one Lord, Jesus Christ,	1 Cor. 8:6; Eph. 4:5–6
the unique[2]	John 1:18; 3:16
Son of God,	Matt. 14:33; 16:16
begotten of the Father before all ages,	John 1:14; 17:5
God of God,	John 1:18; 20:28; 2 Pet. 1:1
Light of Light,	Ps. 27:1; John 8:12; 1 John 1:5
true God of true God,	John 17:1–5
Of one substance with the Father,	John 10:30; 14:10
through whom all things were made,	John 1:3; Col. 1:16; Heb. 1:1–2
who for us and for our salvation	Luke 2:30; 19:10; 1 Tim. 2:4–5

1. See chap. 5, above.
2. Or, Only-begotten.

came down from heaven,
and was incarnate of the Holy Spirit and
  the virgin Mary,
and became man,
and was crucified for us

under Pontius Pilate,
and suffered
and was buried,
and rose again on the third day
according to the Scriptures,
and ascended into heaven,
and sits at the right hand of the Father,
and is coming again in glory
to judge the living and dead,
and of whose kingdom there shall be no
  end;
and [we believe] in the Holy Spirit,
the Lord
and giver of life,
who proceeds from the Father,
who with the Father and the Son is
  worshipped and glorified,
who spoke through the prophets.
And [we believe] in one
holy
catholic

and apostolic church;
we confess one baptism
for the remission of sins;
we look for the resurrection of the dead,
and the life of the age to come.
Amen.

John 6:33, 35, 50; Phil. 2:7
Matt. 1:23; Luke 1:35

John 1:14; 1 John 4:2
Mark 15:25; John 19:16; 1 Cor. 15:3; Phil.
  2:8
Matt. 27:24–27; Luke 23:24
Mark 8:31; Phil. 2:8; Heb. 9:28
Luke 23:53; 1 Cor. 15:4
Luke 24:46; 1 Cor. 15:4
1 Cor. 15:3
Luke 24:51; Acts 1:10
Mark 16:19; Acts 7:55
Matt. 24:27; 1 Thess. 4:16–17; Rev. 1:7
Acts 10:42; Rom. 2:16
Luke 1:33; Heb. 13:8; 2 Pet. 1:11

John 14:26; 20:22; Eph. 1:13
Luke 4:18; Acts 5:3–4
Gen. 1:2; Acts 2:4; 19:6
Matt. 10:20; John 15:26
Matt. 3:16–17; 28:19; 2 Cor. 13:14

1 Sam. 19:20; Ezek. 11:5, 13; Heb. 1:1–3
Matt. 16:18; 1 Cor. 10:17; Eph. 4:13
Rom. 12:1; 1 Cor. 3:17; 1 Pet. 2:5, 9
1 Cor. 4:17b; Eph. 4:4–6, 16; 2 Tim. 2:14;
  Philem. 5
Acts 2:42; Eph. 2:19–22
Acts 2:38; Eph. 4:5
1 Cor. 15:3; Luke 24:26
John 5:29; 11:24; 1 Cor. 15:12–49
Mark 10:29–30
Ps. 106:48; Rev. 22:21

SELECT BIBLIOGRAPHY

There is a strange idea abroad that in every subject the ancient books should only be read by the professionals, and that the amateur should content himself with the modern books. . . . The student is half afraid to meet one of the great philosophers face to face. He feels himself inadequate and thinks that he will not understand him. But if he only knew, the great man, just because of his greatness, is much more intelligible than his modern commentator.

This mistaken preference for the modern books and this shyness of the old ones is nowhere more rampant than in theology.

(C. S. Lewis, Introduction to *St. Athanasius:
On the Incarnation*)

Primary Sources in Translation

Ancient Christian Writers. Ed. J. Quasten and J. C. Plumpe. New York: Newman, 1946–.
Very good English translations and thorough notes to the text.

The Ante-Nicene Fathers. Ed. A. Roberts and J. Donaldson. 10 vols. Grand Rapids: Eerdmans, 1979.
American reprint of the Edinburgh edition, The Ante-Nicene Christian Library (1885–87). This set was reprinted by Hendrickson Publishers in 1994.

The Early Church Fathers. Carol Harrison, gen. ed. London: Routledge, 1996–.
Newly translated texts, some for the first time in English, of leading patristic figures: Irenaeus *(1997),* John Chrysostom *(1999),* Maximus the Confessor *(1996),* Ambrose *(1997),* Origen *(1998),* Cyril of Jerusalem *(2000),* Gregory of Nyssa *(1999),* Cyril of Alexandria *(2000), and others forthcoming.*

Fathers of the Church. New York: Fathers of the Church, 1947–.
Good quality English translations of select works and helpful introductions.

Library of Christian Classics. Ed. J. Baillie, J. McNeill, and H. Van Dussen. Philadelphia: Westminster, 1953–.
   Selected writings, usually entire, from various ancient authors.
The Nicene and Post-Nicene Fathers of the Christian Church. Series 1. Ed. P. Schaff. 14 vols. Series 2. Ed. P. Schaff and H. Wace. 14 vols. Grand Rapids: Eerdmans, 1983–87.
   American reprint of the Edinburgh editions (1886–90, 1890–1900). Now both series 1 and 2 have been reprinted by Hendrickson Publishers.
Sources of Early Christian Thought. W. G. Rusch, gen. ed. Philadelphia: Fortress, 1980–.
   Series of texts thematically arranged according to theological topic: The Trinitarian Controversy *(1980),* The Christological Controversy *(1980),* Theological Anthropology *(1981),* Biblical Interpretation in the Early Church *(1984),* Early Christian Spirituality *(1986),* Understandings of the Church *(1986),* The Early Church and the State *(1982), and* Marriage in the Early Church *(1992).*
The Works of Augustine for the Twenty-first Century. Ed. John E. Rotelle. Brooklyn, NY: New City, 1990–.
   The complete works of Augustine in contemporary translation (still in progress).

Resources for Further Study

Atlas of the Christian Church. Ed. H. Chadwick and E. Evans. New York: Facts on File, 1987.
Atlas of the Early Christian World. Ed. F. van der Meer and C. Mohrmann. London: Nelson, 1958.
The Cambridge History of Early Christian literature. Ed. Frances Young et al. New York: Cambridge University Press, 2004.
The Early Christian World. Ed. Philip F. Eslei. 2 vols. New York: Routledge, 2000.
Encyclopedia of Early Christianity. Ed. E. Ferguson. 2nd ed. New York: Garland, 1993.
Encyclopedia of the Early Church. Trans. A. Walford. 2 vols. New York: Oxford University Press, 1992.
History of Theology: The Patristic Period. Ed. A. Di Berardino and B. Studer. Collegeville, MN: Liturgical Press, 1997.
Kelly, J. N. D. *Early Christian Creeds.* Rev. ed. London: Longman, 1978.
———. *Early Christian Doctrines.* Rev. ed. London: Black, 1977.
Patrology. Ed. J. Quasten. Vols. 1–3. 1950. Repr., Westminster, MD: Newman, 1983. Vol. 4. Ed. A. Di Berardino. 1988.
Ramsey, Boniface. *Beginning to Read the Fathers.* New York: Paulist Press, 1985.

Patristic Interpretation of the Bible

Dawson, David. *Christian Figural Reading and the Fashioning of Identity.* Berkeley: University of California Press, 2002.
Gamble, Harry. *Books and Readers in the Early Church.* New Haven: Yale University Press, 1995.

Gorday, Peter. *Principles of Patristic Exegesis: Romans 9–11 in Origen, John Chrysostom, and Augustine*. New York: Mellen, 1983.

Kannengiesser, Charles. *Handbook of Patristic Exegesis: The Bible in Ancient Christianity*. Leiden: Brill, 2004.

O'Keefe, John, and Russell Reno. *Sanctified Vision: An Introduction to Early Christian Interpretation of the Bible*. Baltimore: Johns Hopkins University Press, 2005.

Simonetti, Manlio. *Biblical Interpretation in the Early Church: A Historical Introduction to Patristic Exegesis*. Edinburgh: T&T Clark, 1994.

General Narratives of the Early Church

Chadwick, Henry. *The Early Church*. New York: Penguin, 1967.

Cross, Frank L. *The Early Christian Fathers*. London: Duckworth, 1960.

Drobner, H. *Fathers of the Church: A Comprehensive Introduction*. Peabody, MA: Hendrickson, 2005.

Frend, W. H. C. *The Rise of Christianity*. Philadelphia: Fortress, 1985.

Gonzalez, Justo L. *The Story of Christianity*. Vol. 1. San Francisco: HarperCollins, 1984.

Hall, Stuart. *Doctrine and Practice in the Early Church*. Grand Rapids: Eerdmans, 1991.

Hinson, E. Glenn. *The Early Church: Origins to the Dawn of the Middle Ages*. Nashville: Abingdon, 1996.

Kelly, Joseph F. *The World of the Early Christians*. Message of the Fathers of the Church 1. Collegeville, MN: Liturgical Press, 1997.

Pelikan, Jaroslav. *The Christian Tradition: A History of the Development of Doctrine*. Vol. 1, *The Emergence of the Catholic Tradition (100–600)*. Chicago: University of Chicago Press, 1971.

Stark, Rodney. *The Rise of Christianity: A Sociologist Reconsiders History*. Princeton, NJ: Princeton University Press, 1996.

The Material Side of Early Christianity

Finney, Paul C. *The Invisible God: The Earliest Christians on Art*. Oxford: Oxford University Press, 1994.

Frend, W. H. C. *The Archaeology of Early Christianity: A History*. Minneapolis: Fortress, 1996.

Jensen, Robin. *Understanding Early Christian Art*. New York: Routledge, 2000.

Snyder, Graydon F. *Ante pacem: Archaeological Evidence of Church Life before Constantine*. Rev. ed. Macon, GA: Mercer University Press, 2003.

Stevenson, James. *The Catacombs: Rediscovered Monuments of Early Christianity*. London: Thames & Hudson, 1979.

Printed and bound by CPI Group (UK) Ltd, Croydon, CR0 4YY

13/04/2025

14656460-0005